Latin Primer
Book I

TEACHER'S EDITION

by Martha Wilson

Canon Press
Moscow, Idaho

The Mars Hill Textbook Series

Introductory Logic, Doug Wilson & James B. Nance
Introductory Logic: Video Tapes featuring James B. Nance
Introductory Logic: Teacher Training Video Tapes featuring James B. Nance

Intermediate Logic, James B. Nance
Intermediate Logic: Video Tapes featuring James B. Nance
Intermediate Logic: Teacher Training Video Tapes featuring James B. Nance

Latin Primer: Book I, Martha Wilson
Latin Primer I: Video Tapes featuring Julie Garfield
Latin Primer I: Audio Pronunciation Tape featuring Julie Garfield

Latin Primer: Book II, Martha Wilson
Latin Primer II: Video Tapes featuring Julie Garfield
Latin Primer II: Audio Pronunciation Tape featuring Julie Garfield

Latin Primer: Book III, Martha Wilson
Latin Primer III: Video Tapes featuring Julie Garfield
Latin Primer III: Audio Pronunciation Tape featuring Julie Garfield

Latin Grammar: Book I, Doug Wilson & Karen Craig
Latin Grammar: Book II, Karen Craig

Matin Latin Book I, Karen Craig
Matin Latin Flashcards Book I, Karen Craig
Matin Latin Worksheet Pkt. Book I, Karen Craig
Matin Latin I: Video Tapes featuring Karen Craig

Matin Latin Book II, Karen Craig
Matin Latin Flashcards Book II, Karen Craig
Matin Latin Worksheet Pkt. Book II, Karen Craig
Matin Latin II: Video Tapes featuring Karen Craig

Martha Wilson, Latin Primer Book I *(Teacher's Edition)*
©1992 by Martha Wilson
First Edition 1992
Second Edition 2001
Published by Canon Press, P.O. Box 8729, Moscow, ID 83843
800-488-2034 http://www.canonpress.org

Printed in the United States of America

ISBN: 1-885767-31-5

TABLE OF CONTENTS

TABLE OF CONTENTS

ACKNOWLEDGMENTS

There are many people who showed me kindness and gave me help in this project. There are some without whom it might never have gone to print:

My husband Jeff, who acquired an unfinished Latin book along with his new bride and gave me much encouragement and help;

Our parents, who have given us more than can be told;

Doug Wilson, who got me started in Latin, the teaching of Latin, and the writing of this book;

Tom Garfield, my principal for six years at Logos School;

Evan and Leslie Wilson, who provided a happy home and one conducive to this sort of thing;

Fred and Lynaire Banks, who helped me in the work in thoughtful ways;

Terry Morin, a very patient editor;

The people of Logos School, those servants who in their work and godliness have blessed many, including me, and the students, who made teaching a delight.

non nobis, Domine,
non nobis sed nomini tuo da gloriam

SOURCES AND HELPS

American Heritage Dictionary of the English Language, new college edition ed. William Morris. Boston: Houghton Mifflin, 1976. This was my basic reference English dictionary and one I would recommend for the teaching of Latin. My main use for it was in confirming and defining derivatives.

Biblia Sacra Vulgata, ed. Robertus Weber. Wurtttembergische Bibelanstalt Stuttgart, Zweite, verbesserte Auflage 1975. I used this and perhaps other versions for scripture quotations. I think the editor is correctly cited, but the printing information is in German:

Brunel, Donald J.,Jr. *Basic Latin Vocabulary* American Classical League, 1989. In the later stages of developing the curriculum, this was my basic source for choosing and defining vocabulary.

Buehner, William J., and John W. Ambrose. *Introduction to Preparatory Latin, Book I*, 2nd ed. Wellesley Hills: Independent School Press, 1977.

Cassell's Latin and English Dictionary, compiled by D.P. Simpson. New York: Macmillan Publishing, 1987. This is my most commonly used Latin dictionary, as well as the one the students used in their work.

Ehrlich, Eugene. *Amo, Amas, Amat, and More.* New York: Harper and Row, 1985.

Schaeffer, Rudolph F. *Latin English Derivative Dictionary*, ed. W. C. Carr. American Classical League

Wheelock, Frederic M. *Latin An Introductory Course Based on Ancient Authors* 3rd ed. New York: Harper and Row, 1963. I depended upon this for Latin grammar and I would recommend it for teachers of Latin who need more of a Latin background.

HOW TO USE THIS BOOK

This copy of the Teacher's Edition is revised to more closely follow the path of the Student Edition. The first part of this book (pgs. 10 through 102) provides an exact mirror of the Student Edition.

In addition, the first part also corresponds directly to the Video Tape Series. We enthusiastically encourage use of the videos for Latin teachers using the workbooks for the first time, as many of the video lessons provide supplemental information not provided in the Teacher's book. Featuring Julie Garfield, the videos take students through each lesson, beginning with recitation of the word lists and chants. Word pronunciation and chant review is provided in a "classroom" setting, with other students participating.

The second part of the book, beginning on page 104, provides teaching tools, including an overview of chants, general grammar, weekly lessons, examinations, and word lists. These tools will provide the Classroom or Homeschool teacher with the proficiency to introduce beginning Latin with confidence.

It's important to note that Latin Primer 1 covers the very basics of classical Latin in the pattern of the trivium model of education. The trivium sees students developing through stages of learning, namely, poll-parrot, pert, and rhetorical stages, corresponding roughly to elementary (ages five through ten), junior high, and high school. Latin Primer 1 is designed for the poll-parrot stage in which children love to chant and memorize. According to the trivium as conceived by Dorothy Sayers, the poll-parrot stage is the time to store away large amounts of information which the students do not yet fully understand. Understanding comes at the next stage. Therefore, they memorize vocabulary, verb and noun endings, etc., whereas other language paths aim to do it all at the same time. The ease of a trivium approach to Latin is just this focus on absorbing the frame now and understanding it later. This will seem odd at first, but it has a long pedigree.

GOALS OF FIRST YEAR LATIN

The goals of this first year Latin study are:

1) to pronounce correctly Latin letters and words,

2) to acquire a vocabulary of approximately 350 words,

3) to recognize Latin derivatives in English, develop facility in the use of a dictionary for etymology, to grow in English vocabulary,

4) to understand and use grammar in Latin and English to the following extent:

   - Latin: declension of first and second declension nouns, conjugation of first and second conjugation verbs,

   - English and Latin: concepts of singular and plural; tense; nouns, verbs, and adjectives; person; word order,

5) to memorize beginning Latin paradigms in chants,

6) to be exposed to Latin quotes and expressions,

7) to do simple translation work,

8) and to acquire some knowledge of Roman history.

Valete,
Martha Wilson

Week 1

Word List:

1. amō	I love	
2. videō	I see	
3. caput	head	
4. et	and	

Chant:

amō	amāmus
amās	amātis
amat	amant

Quotation:

"et cetera"—and the rest

Week 2

Word List:

1.	laudō	I praise
2.	sum	I am
3.	cogitō	I think
4.	vīvō	I live
5.	audiō	I hear
6.	amīcus	friend
7.	puer	boy
8.	puella	girl
9.	salvē	Good day! (Be well)
10.	valē	Good bye! (Be well)
11.	vir	man
12.	canis	dog
13.	mater	mother
14.	pater	father
15.	domus	house *or* home

Chant:

sum	sumus
es	estis
est	sunt

Quotation:

"Cave canem"—Beware of the dog

Week 3

Word List:

1.	creō	I create
2.	dō	I give
3.	clamō	I shout
4.	Deus	God
5.	lux	light
6.	avis	bird
7.	sōl	sun
8.	lūna	moon
9.	mare	sea
10.	caelum	sky
11.	terra	earth
12.	stella	star
13.	flūmen	river
14.	mons	mountain
15.	nihil	nothing

Chant:

ō	mus
s	tis
t	nt

Quotation:

"In principio creavit Deus caelum et terram."

In the beginning God created the heavens and the earth.

Week 4

Word List:

1.	dīrigō	I direct
2.	doceō	I teach
3.	dēmonstrō	I show
4.	portō	I carry
5.	laborō	I work
6.	lūdus	game *or* school
7.	magister	teacher
8.	magistra	woman teacher
9.	discipulus	student
10.	discipula	girl student
11.	liber	book
12.	bonus	good
13.	parvus	little
14.	magnus	large
15.	semper	always

Chant:

bō	bimus
bis	bitis
bit	bunt

Quotation:

"semper fidelis"—always faithful

Week 5

Word List:

1.	administrō	I help *or* manage
2.	mūtō	I change
3.	ōrō	I pray
4.	tardō	I delay
5.	līberō	I set free
6.	oculus	eye
7.	pēs	foot
8.	crūs	leg
9.	bracchium	arm
10.	ōs	mouth
11.	corpus	body
12.	manus	hand
13.	novus	new
14.	malus	bad *or* evil
15.	in	in *or* into

Chant: No new chant this week.

Quotation:

         "dirigo"—I direct

Week 6

Word List:

1.	vocō	I call
2.	spērō	I hope
3.	scrībō	I write
4.	currō	I run
5.	faciō	I make *or* do
6.	fēmina	woman
7.	frāter	brother
8.	soror	sister
9.	nomen	name
10.	arbor	tree
11.	silva	forest
12.	insula	island
13.	collis	hill
14.	suprā	above
15.	sub	below

Chant:

bam	bāmus
bās	bātis
bat	bant

Quotation:

"Dum spiro, spero"—While I breathe, I hope

(Motto for state of South Carolina)

Week 7

Word List:

1.	dēspērō	I despair of
2.	exspectō	I wait for
3.	imperō	I order
4.	cūrō	I care for
5.	simulō	I pretend

Chant: No new chant this week.

Quotation: No quotation this week.

Week 8

Word List:

1.	habeō	I have *or* hold
2.	moveō	I move
3.	valeō	I am well
4.	sedeō	I sit
5.	navigō	I sail
6.	patria	native land
7.	nauta	sailor
8.	navis	ship
9.	aqua	water
10.	labor	work, toil
11.	diēs	day
12.	vesper	evening, evening star
13.	nox	night
14.	ex	out of
15.	saepe	often

Chant:

videō	vidēmus
vidēs	vidētis
videt	vident

Quotation:

"ex libris"—from the books

Week 9

Word List:

1.	capiō	I take *or* capture
2.	timeō	I fear
3.	terreō	I frighten
4.	vincō	I conquer
5.	oppugnō	I attack
6.	mīles	soldier
7.	equus	horse
8.	perīculum	danger
9.	metus	fear
10.	cōpiae	troops
11.	ignis	fire
12.	bellum	war
13.	gladius	sword
14.	castellum	castle
15.	contrā	against

Chant:

possum	possumus
potes	potestis
potest	possunt

Quotation:

"ante bellum"—before the war

Week 10

Word List:

1.	agō	I do, act
2.	regō	I rule
3.	precor	I pray
4.	dēbeō	I owe *or* ought
5.	servō	I save
6.	rēx	king
7.	lex	law
8.	vīta	life
9.	crux	cross
10.	homō	man, human being
11.	familia	household
12.	fīlius	son
13.	fīlia	daughter
14.	glōria	fame, glory
15.	nunc	now

Chant:

a	ae
ae	ārum
ae	īs
am	ās
ā	īs

Quotation:

P.S. "post scriptum"—written afterwards

Week 11

Word List:

1.	ūnus	one
2.	duo	two
3.	trēs	three
4.	quattuor	four
5.	quinque	five
6.	sex	six
7.	septem	seven
8.	octō	eight
9.	novem	nine
10.	decem	ten
11.	centum	a hundred
12.	mille	a thousand
13.	pecūnia	money
14.	numerus	number
15.	paucī	few

Chant:

us	ī
ī	ōrum
ō	īs
um	ōs
ō	īs

Quotation:

"e plurbis unum"—out of many, one (or) one out of many

Week 12

Word List:

1.	stō	I stand
2.	audeō	I dare
3.	volō	I fly
4.	ponō	I put *or* place
5.	dubitō	I doubt
6.	dominus	lord *or* master
7.	ager	field
8.	servus	slave
9.	sōlum	floor *or* ground
10.	porta	door *or* gate
11.	mensa	table
12.	grātiae	thanks
13.	difficilis	difficult
14.	facilis	easy
15.	ad	to, toward

Chant:

ī	imus
istī	istis
it	ērunt

Quotation:

A.D. "Anno Domini"—In the year of our Lord

Week 13

Word List:

1.	teneō	I hold *or* possess
2.	pareō	I obey
3.	moneō	I warn
4.	spectō	I look at
5.	doleō	I grieve
6.	digitus	finger
7.	cor	heart
8.	capillus	hair
9.	auris	ear
10.	faciēs	face
11.	mens	mind
12.	longus	long
13.	dulcis	sweet
14.	fortis	strong *or* brave
15.	gratiās agō	thanks!

Chant:

erō	erimus
eris	eritis
erit	erint

Quotation:

"Gloria in excelsis Deo"—Glory to Go in the highest

Week 14

Word List:

1.	dēleō	I destroy
2.	necō	I kill
3.	occupō	I seize
4.	respondeō	I answer
5.	fleō	I weep

Chant: No new chant this week.

Quotation: No quotation this week.

Week 15

Word List:

1.	iuvō	I help
2.	communicō	I share
3.	augeō	I increase
4.	mereō	I deserve
5.	maneō	I remain
6.	aedificium	building
7.	cīvis	citizen
8.	urbs	city
9.	oppidum	town
10.	via	road, way
11.	Rōma	Rome
12.	Italia	Italy
13.	Gallia	Gaul
14.	Hispānia	Spain
15.	Germānia	Germany

Chant:

eram	erāmus
erās	erātis
erat	erant

Quotation:

"cum laude"—with praise

Week 16

Word List:

1.	vīcus	village
2.	captīvus	captive
3.	mūrus	wall
4.	praefectus	officer
5.	praeda	booty
6.	moenia	fortifications, city walls
7.	campus	level area, athletic field
8.	putō	I think
9.	parō	I prepare
10.	recuperō	I recover
11.	superō	I conquer
12.	exerceō	I train, exercise
13.	princeps	chief
14.	vulnus	wound
15.	castra	camp

Chant:

r	mur
ris	minī
tur	ntur

Quotation:

"Hannibal ad portas"—Hannibal is at the gates

Week 17

Word List:

1.	nuntius	message *or* messenger
2.	iniūria	injury
3.	triumphus	triumph
4.	fāma	report, reputation
5.	sagitta	arrow
6.	sīca	dagger
7.	pugna	fight
8.	lēgātus	lieutenant
9.	exercitus	army
10.	hostis	enemy
11.	noceō	I harm
12.	iubeō	I order
13.	perturbō	I confuse
14.	ferus	fierce
15.	antīquus	ancient

Chant:

bor	bimur
beris	biminī
bitur	buntur

Quotation:

"terra incognita"—unknown land

Week 18

Word List:

1.	populus, ī	people, nation
2.	colōnus, ī	settler
3.	socius, ī	partner *or* associate
4.	rēgīna, ae	queen
5.	corōna, ae	crown
6.	dux	leader
7.	gens	tribe
8.	probō	I approve
9.	negō	I deny
10.	lēgō	I appoint
11.	prohibeō	I prevent
12.	recusō	I refuse
13.	nōn	not
14.	potens	powerful
15.	miser	unhappy, wretched, miserable

Chant:

bār	bāmur
bāris	bāminī
bātur	bantur

Quotation:

"Veni, vidi, vici"—I came, I saw, I conquered

Week 19

Word List:

1.	lupus, ī	wolf
2.	nimbus, ī	cloud
3.	taurus, ī	bull
4.	aura, ae	breeze
5.	herba, ae	herb, plant
6.	spēlunca, ae	cave
7.	aquila, ae	eagle
8.	ripa, ae	bank
9.	flōreō	I flourish
10.	explōrō	I find out
11.	occultō	I hide
12.	dēlectō	I delight
13.	clam	secretly
14.	bene	well
15.	satis	enough

Chant: No new chant this week.

Quotation:

"et tu, Brute"—Even you, Brutus

Week 20

Word List:

1.	verbum, ī	word
2.	dōnum, ī	gift
3.	saxum, ī	rock
4.	signum, ī	sign
5.	regnum, ī	kingdom
6.	pābulum, ī	fodder, food for animals
7.	scūtum, ī	shield
8.	stagnum, ī	pond
9.	tēlum, ī	weapon
10.	pīlum, ī	javelin
11.	auxilium, ī	help, aid
12.	praemium, ī	reward
13.	beneficium, ī	kindness
14.	folium, ī	leaf
15.	silentium, ī	silence

Chant:

um	a
ī	ōrum
ō	īs
um	a
ō	īs

Quotation:

"excelsior"—even higher

(Motto for the state of New York)

Week 21

Word List:

1.	geminus, ī	twin
2.	ursa, ae *or* ursus, ī	bear
3.	scorpius, ī	scorpion
4.	lībra, ae	pair of scales
5.	aquārius, ī	water-carrier
6.	sagittārius, ī	archer
7.	aurīga, ae	charioteer
8.	aurōra, ae	dawn
9.	leō	lion
10.	piscis	fish
11.	virgō	maiden
12.	ariēs	ram
13.	cancer	crab
14.	māior	greater
15.	minor	smaller

Extra Credit

1.	Borēus	northern
2.	austrīlis	southern

Chant: No new chant this week.

Quotation: No quotation this week.

Week 22

Word List:

1.	appellō	I name
2.	rogō	I ask
3.	errō	I wander
4.	recitō	I read aloud
5.	placeō	I please
6.	avus, ī	grandfather
7.	adulēscēns	young man
8.	animus, ī	mind
9.	patientia, ae	patience
10.	disciplīna, ae	instruction, training
11.	beātus, a, um	happy, blessed
12.	stultus, a, um	foolish
13.	honestus, a, um	honorable
14.	improbus, a, um	wicked
15.	contentus, a, um	satisfied, content

Chant:

hic ▶	haec ▶	hoc
huius ▶	huius ▶	huius
huic ▶	huic ▶	huic
hunc ▶	hanc ▶	hoc
hōc ▶	hāc ▶	hōc

Quotation:

"Cogito ergo sum"—I think therefore I am

Week 23

Word List:

1.	ancora, ae	anchor
2.	rēmus, ī	oar
3.	ventus, ī	wind
4.	vēlum, ī	sail
5.	ōra, ae	shore
6.	unda, ae	wave
7.	tempestās	weather, storm
8.	iter	journey
9.	classis	fleet (of ships)
10.	portus	harbor
11.	pons	bridge
12.	nō	I swim
13.	aequus, a, um	level, even, calm
14.	lātus, a, um	wide, broad
15.	prope	near

Chant:

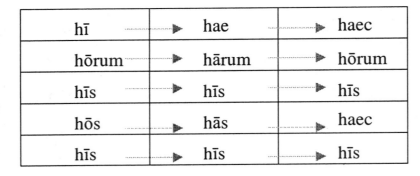

Quotation:

"Deo volente"—God willing

Week 24

Word List:

1.	Iesus	Jesus
2.	Christus, ī	Christ
3.	apostolus, ī	apostle
4.	poena, ae	penalty, punishment
5.	evangelium, ī	good news
6.	ecclēsia, ae	church
7.	Biblia Sacra	Holy Bible
8.	pax	peace
9.	mors	death
10.	fidēs	faith
11.	spēs	hope
12.	vērus, a, um	true
13.	vīvus, a, um	living
14.	crēdō	I believe
15.	praedicō	I proclaim

Chant:

ego	nōs		tu	vōs
meī	nostrum		tuī	vestrum
mihi	nōbīs		tibi	vōbīs
mē	nōs		tē	vōs
mē	nōbīs		tē	vōbīs

Quotation:

"Iesus Rex Iudaeorum"—Jesus, King of the Jews

Week 25

Word List:

1.	agricola, ae	farmer
2.	villa, ae	farmhouse, country house
3.	hortus, ī	garden
4.	stabulum, ī	stall, stable
5.	fossa, ae	ditch
6.	cibus, ī	food
7.	vīnum, ī	wine
8.	animal	animal
9.	famēs	hunger, famine, starvation
10.	pastor	shepherd
11.	sēmen	seed
12.	pulvis	dirt, dust, powder
13.	albus, a, um	white
14.	vulnerō	I wound
15.	serō	I sow, plant

Chant:　　　　No new chant this week.

Quotation:

"Sic semper tyrannis"—Thus always to tyrants

(Motto for the state of Virginia)

Week 26

Word List:

1.	toga, ae	toga
2.	īra, ae	anger
3.	forum, ī	public square, marketplace
4.	sacculus, ī	little bag
5.	lingua, ae	language
6.	sententia, ae	opinion
7.	vox	voice
8.	rēs	thing
9.	postulō	I demand
10.	vītō	I avoid
11.	censeō	I estimate
12.	aliēnus, a, um	foreign
13.	mīrus, a, um	strange, wonderful
14.	mediocris	ordinary
15.	inter	between

Chant: No new chant this week.

Quotation:

"In hoc signo vinces"—In this sign you will conquer

Week 27

Word List:

1.	annus, ī	year
2.	tempus	time
3.	hora, ae	hour
4.	mensis	month
5.	hodiē	today
6.	merīdiēs	noon
7.	ante	before
8.	post	after
9.	heri	yesterday
10.	crās	tomorrow
11.	multus, a, um	much, many
12.	prīmus, a, um	first
13.	sciō	I know
14.	ecce	behold!
15.	fīnis	the end

Chant: No new chant this week.

Quotation:

"ante meridiem"—"post meridiem"

before noon—after noon

CHANT CHARTS

The chants in the section are grouped according to Parts of Speech

Verb Chant

I love

amō	amāmus
amās	amātis
amat	amant

Present Active Verb Endings

ō	mus
s	tis
t	nt

I see

videō	vidēmus
vidēs	vidētis
videt	vident

Future Active Verb Endings

bō	bimus
bis	bitis
bit	bunt

I am

sum	sumus
es	estis
est	sunt

Imperfect Tense Verb Endings

bam	bāmus
bās	bātis
bat	bant

To be able

possum	possumus
potes	potestis
potest	possunt

Perfect Tense Verb Endings

ī	imus
istī	istis
it	ērunt

Future Perfect Active Verb Endings

erō	erimus
eris	eritis
erit	erint

Plural Perfect Active Verb Endings

eram	erāmus
erās	erātis
erat	erant

Present Passive Verb Endings

r	mur
ris	minī
tur	ntur

Verb Chant Chart

Future Passive Verb Endings

bor	bimur
beris	biminī
bitur	buntur

Imperfect Passive Verb Endings

bār	bāmur
bāris	bāminī
bātur	bantur

Noun Chant Chart

First Declension

a	ae
ae	ārum
ae	īs
am	ās
ā	īs

Second Declension

us	ī
ī	orum
ō	īs
um	ōs
ō	īs

Second Declension Neuter

um	a
ī	ōrum
ō	īs
um	a
ō	īs

Pronoun Chant Chart

Singular "this"

hic	haec	hoc
huius	huius	huius
huic	huic	huic
hunc	hanc	hoc
hōc	hāc	hōc

Plural "these"

hī	hae	haec
hōrum	hārum	hōrum
hīs	hīs	hīs
hōs	hās	haec
hīs	hīs	hīs

Pronouns "I *and* us"

ego	nōs
meī	nostrum
mihi	nōbīs
mē	nōs
mē	nōbīs

Pronouns "you *and* we"

tū	vōs
tuī	vestrum
tibi	vōbīs
tē	vōs
tē	vōbīs

The chants in this section are listed in chant order.

Chants

Present Tense (Active) — First Conjugation (or) "a" family

	Singular	**Plural**
1st	amō	amāmus
2nd	amās	amātis
3rd	amat	amant

I love	we love
you love	you (all) love
he, she, it loves	they love

Present Tense — Irregular (Conjugation of I am)

	Singular	**Plural**
1st	sum	sumus
2nd	es	estis
3rd	est	sunt

I am	we are
you are	you (all) are
he, she or it is	they are

Present Tense (Active) Verb Endings

	Singular	**Plural**
1st	ō	mus
2nd	s	tis
3rd	t	nt

I	we
you	you (all)
he, she or it	they

Future Tense (Active) Verb Endings

	Singular	**Plural**
1st	bō	bimus
2nd	bis	bitis
3rd	bit	bunt

I	we
you	you (all)
he, she or it	they

Imperfect Tense (Active) Verb Endings

	Singular	Plural
1st	bam	bāmus
2nd	bās	bātis
3rd	bat	bant

	I	we
	you	you (all)
	he, she or it	they

Present Tense (Active) — Second Conjugation (or) "e" family

	Singular	Plural
1st	videō	vidēmus
2nd	vidēs	vidētis
3rd	videt	vident

	I see	we see
	you see	you (all) see
	he, she, it sees	they see

Present Tense — Irregular (Conjugation of "I am able")

	Singular	Plural
1st	possum	possumus
2nd	potes	potestis
3rd	potest	possunt

	I am able	we are able
	you are able	you (all) are able
	he, she, it is able	they are able

First Declension (or) "a" Family (Noun Endings)

	Singular	Plural
Nom	a	ae
Gen	ae	ārum
Dat.	ae	īs
Acc.	am	ās
Abl.	ā	īs

a noun	the nouns
of the noun, the noun's	of the nouns, the noun's
to / for the noun	to / for the nouns
the noun (as direct object)	the nouns(as direct object)
from / by / with	from / by / with the nouns

Second Declension (or) "us" Family (Noun Endings)

	Singular	Plural		
Nom	us	ī	a noun	the nouns
Gen	ī	orum	of the noun, the noun's	of the nouns, the noun's
Dat.	ō	īs	to / for the noun	to / for the nouns
Acc.	um	ōs	the noun (as direct object)	the nouns(as direct object)
Abl.	ō	īs	from / by / with	from / by / with the nouns

Perfect Tense — Active (Verb Endings)

	Singular	Plural		
1st	ī	imus	I	we
2nd	istī	istis	you	you (all)
3rd	it	erunt	he, she, it	they

Future Perfect Tense — Active (Verb Endings)

	Singular	Plural		
1st	erō	erimus	I	we
2nd	eris	eritis	you	you (all)
3rd	erit	erint	he, she, it	they

Pluperfect Tense — Active (Verb Endings)

	Singular	Plural		
1st	eram	erāmus	I	we
2nd	erās	erātis	you	you (all)
3rd	erat	erant	he, she, it	they

Present Tense — Passive (Verb Endings)

	Singular	Plural
1st	r	mur
2nd	ris	minī
3rd	tur	ntur

I	we
you	you (all)
he, she, it	they

Future Tense — Passive (Verb Endings)

	Singular	Plural
1st	bor	bimur
2nd	beris	biminī
3rd	bitur	buntur

I	we
you	you (all)
he, she, it	they

Future Tense — Passive (Verb Endings)

	Singular	Plural
1st	bār	bāmur
2nd	bāris	bāminī
3rd	bātur	bantur

I	we
you	you (all)
he, she, it	they

Second Declension Neuter (or) "um" Family (Noun Endings)

	Singular	Plural
Nom	um	a
Gen	ī	ōrum
Dat.	ō	īs
Acc.	um	a
Abl.	ō	īs

a noun	the nouns
of the noun, the noun's	of the nouns, the noun's
to / for the noun	to / for the nouns
the noun (as direct object)	the nouns(as direct object)
from / by / with	from / by / with the nouns

Singular (Pronoun) "this"

	Masculine	Feminine	Neuter
Nom	hic	haec	hoc
Gen	huius	huius	huius
Dat.	huic	huic	huic
Acc.	hunc	hanc	hoc
Abl.	hōc	hāc	hōc

Plural (Pronoun) "these"

	Masculine	Feminine	Neuter
Nom	hī	hae	haec
Gen	hōrum	hārum	hōrum
Dat.	hīs	hīs	hīs
Acc.	hōs	hās	haec
Abl.	hīs	hīs	hīs

Pronouns "I" and "us"

	Singular	Plural		I	we
Nom	ego	nōs		I	we
Gen	meī	nostrum		of me	of us
Dat.	mihi	nōbīs		to / for me	to / for us
Acc.	mē	nōs		me	is
Abl.	mē	nōbīs		by, with, from me	by, with, from us

Pronouns "you" and "we"

	Singular	Plural		you	you (plural)
Nom	tū	vōs		you	you (plural)
Gen	tuī	vestrum		of you	of you
Dat.	tibi	vōbīs		to / for you	to / for you
Acc.	tē	vōs		you	you
Abl.	tē	vōbīs		by, with, from you	by, with, from you

WORKSHEETS

Weekly Worksheet 1

A) Write the chant for this week in the box (pg. 10). The verb *amō* is first conjugation (or) "a" family.

I love	amō	amāmus	we love
you love	amās	amātis	you (all) love
he, she, it loves	amat	amant	they love

B) Translate each word on its line. The one in italics will probably be harder because you'll need to translate it from English into Latin.

amō   <u>I love</u>   caput   <u>head</u>

et   <u>and</u>   *I see*   <u>*videō*</u>

C) Fill in these blanks telling about derivatives of this week's words. A derivative is an English word that comes from Latin. It must meet at least two qualifications:
> 1) similar (like) spelling   2) similar (like) meaning

- The English word *amateur* comes from the Latin word <u>amō</u>.

- An *amateur* is a person who does something because he <u>loves</u> it, rather than for money.

- The English word *evident* comes from the Latin word <u>videō</u>.

- If something is *evident,* you can easily <u>see</u> it.

D) Fill in the blanks about the quotation you learned this week (pg. 10).

- *etc.* is an abbreviation for <u>et cetera</u> which means <u>and the rest</u>.

Weekly Worksheet 2

A) Conjugate "laudō" in the box on the left and translate it in the box on the right.

It is a first conjugation(or) "a" family verb just like "amō." When you conjugate, you put endings on the words to change their form. (eg. I praise, you praise, we praise)

laudō	laudāmus
laudās	laudātis
laudat	laudant

I praise	we praise
you praise	you (all) praise
he, she, it praises	they praise

B) Translate these words from this week's word list (pg. 11). Some will need to be translated from English to Latin. When you translate a word you give the meaning.

laudō	I praise	vīvō	I live
domus	house *or* home	cogitō	I think
sum	I am	puer	boy
puella	girl	salvē	Good Day! (Be well)
valē	Good Bye! (Be well)	audiō	I hear
canis	dog	*mother*	*mater*
father	*pater*	*man*	*vir*
friend	*amicus*		

C) Fill in these blanks telling about derivatives of this week's words.

- The English word *maternal* comes from the Latin word <u>mater</u>.

- *Maternal* love is the love of a <u>mother</u>.

- There is a hymn that begins with these words: "All glory, laud, and honor to Thee, Redeemer, King." What do you think the word *laud* means? <u>praise</u>

D) Write and translate the chant for this week.

sum	sumus		I am	we are
es	estis		you are	you (all) are
est	sunt		he, she, it is	they are

E) Fill in the blanks.

Italian, French, Spanish, Portuguese, and Romanian are languages spoken today in different parts of the world. They are called <u>Romance</u> languages because they come from the language of the Romans. The language of the Romans was <u>Latin</u>. What is the Spanish word for "friend"? <u>amigo</u>

F) The quotation for this week is "Cave canem." Draw a picture using the words in the picture to show your understanding of the quotation. (A drawing page is provided on pg. 126.)

Weekly Worksheet 3

A) Write and translate the chant for this week. This chant shows us the part of a verb that tells us who is doing what.

I	ō	mus	we
you	s	tis	you (all)
he, she, it	t	nt	they

B) Underline the endings of the <u>verbs</u> (the verbs are called personal endings because they show the person who is "doing"). Then translate each verb on the corresponding line.

amā<u>mus</u>	we love
clama<u>nt</u>	they shout
d<u>ō</u>	I give
cogitā<u>tis</u>	you (all) think
laudā<u>s</u>	you praise
crea<u>t</u>	he, she, or it creates

C) Translate the following words from this week's word list (pg. 12).

lux	light	Deus	God
luna	moon	nihil	nothing
flūmen	river	mons	mountain
caelum	sky	creō	I create
clamō	I shout	dō	I give
avis	bird	*star*	*stella*
sea	*mare*	*earth*	*terra*
sun	*sol*		

D) Translate this quotation taken from the Latin Bible.

"In principio creavit Deus caelum et terram."

In the beginning God created the heavens and the earth.

E) Translate these words from word lists 1 and 2 (pgs. 10 and 11).

audiō	I hear	vivō	I live
caput	head	domus	house *or* home
man	*vir*	*and*	*et*

Weekly Worksheet 4

A) Conjugate the verbs in the boxes on the left and then translate them in boxes to the right. These are all first-conjugation verbs in the "a" family.

portō	portāmus		I carry	we carry
portās	portātis		you carry	you (all) carry
portat.	portant		he, she, or it carries	they carry

laborō	laborāmus		I work	we work
laborās	laborātis		you work	you (all) work
laborat	laborant		he, she, or it works	they work

dō	dāmus		I give	we give
dās	dātis		you give	you (all) give
dat	dant		he, she, or it gives	they give

B) The word *portō* has many derivatives in English. List as many as you can. Think about what they have to do with "carrying." <u><u>Double underline</u></u> one of them and on the bottom line tell what it has to do with carrying.

portage, transportation, portable, important, portfolio

portmanteau, import, export, deport, report, rapport, <u>porter</u>

The type that carries luggage and not a doorman.

C) "Semper Fidelis" is the motto of the United States Marine Corps.

What does it mean? <u>"Always faithful"</u>

Besides having a Latin motto, the Marine Corps has a name that comes from Latin words. *Corps* comes from a word that you will learn next week. What Latin word does *marine* come from? <u>mare</u>

D) Write the chant for this week (pg. 13).

bō	bimus
bis	bitis
bit	bunt

Weekly Worksheet 5

	Singular		Plural	
1st	ō	I	mus	we
2nd	s	you	tis	you all
3rd	t	he, she, it	nt	they

A) Underline the endings on these verbs. Then translate the verbs and state whether they are first, second, or third-person.

administrō	I help *or* manage	First
ōrat	he, she, or it prays	Third
līberat	he, she, or it sets free	Third
tardāmus	we delay	First
mūtant	they change	Third
cogitat	he, she, or it thinks	Third

B) Fill in the blanks in these sentences about derivatives of this week's words.

- *Malign, malignant, malevolence, malaria, malady, malpractice, malicious,* and *malice* are just some of the English words that come from <u>malus</u>. To have *malice* toward someone is to want <u>bad</u> things to happen to him.

- *Novice* comes from the Latin word <u>novus</u> which means <u>new</u>. If someone is a *novice,* he is a beginner. As a Latin scholar, you are a <u>novice</u>.

- *Manual* comes from <u>manus</u>. A car with a *manual* transmission is shifted by <u>hand</u>.

C) Draw a picture of a person and label these *corpus* parts: *oculus, crūs, pēs, ōs, bracchium,* and *manus.* (A drawing page is provided on pg. 127.)

D) Give the Latin motto of the state of Maine, and its translation.

Dirigō—I direct

E) In the boxes below, write the chants you've learned the first four weeks and their meanings.

amō	amāmus
amās	amātis
amat	amant

I love	we love
you love	you (all) love
he, she, it loves	they love

sum	sumus
es	estis
est	sunt

I am	we are
you are	you (all) are
he, she, it is	they are

ō	mus
s	tis
t	nt

I	we
you	you (all)
he, she, *or* it	they

bō	bimus
bis	bitis
bit	bunt

I	we
you	you (all)
he, she, *or* it	they

Weekly Worksheet 6

A) Conjugate and translate the verbs in the boxes on the left and then translate them in the boxes to the right. The verbs are all first conjugation (or) "a" family.

spērō	spērāmus
spērās	spērātis
spērat	spērant

I hope	we hope
you hope	you (all) hope
he, she, it hopes	they hope

vocō	vocāmus
vocās	vocātis
vocat	vocant

I call	we call
you call	you (all) call
he, she, it calls	they call

mūtō	mūtāmus
mūtās	mūtātis
mūt	mūtant

I change	we change
you change	you (all) change
he, she, it changes	they change

B) Translate the following verbs from this week's word list (pg. 15).

frāter	brother	soror	sister
spērō	I hope	faciō	I make *or* do
collis	hill	suprā	above
scrībō	I write	insula	island
arbor	tree	currō	I run
woman	*fēmina*	*I call*	*vocō*
name	*nomen*	*forest*	*silva*

C) Derivatives: Which Latin words do these English words come from?

- The English word *arboretum* comes from <u>arbor</u>. An *arboretum* is a place which has rare <u>trees</u> to look at and study.

- *Submarine* comes from two Latin words and tells us that a *submarine* can travel <u>under</u> the <u>sea</u>.

- *Peninsula* also comes from two Latin words: *paene* which means "almost" and *insula* which means <u>island</u>. Therefore, a peninsula is <u>almost an island</u>.

D) Write the chant for this week (pg. 15).

bam	bāmus
bās	bātis
bat	bant

E) Give the translation for South Carolina's motto, "Dum spiro, spero."

While I breathe, I hope

Weekly Worksheet 7

(Test Practice / Weeks 1–7)

A) Conjugate the verbs in the boxes on the left and then translate them in boxes to the right.

cūrō	cūrāmus
cūrās	cūrātis
cūrat	cūrant

I care for	we care for
you care for	you (all) care for
he, she, it cares for	they care for

imperō	imperāmus
imperās	imperātis
imperat	imperant

I order	we order
you order	you (all) order
he, she, it orders	they order

B) Translate these verbs from the first seven word lists. When you translate you give the meaning of the word.

portātis	you (all) carry
laborant	they work
stimulat	he, she, *or* it pretends
dēspērāmus	we despair of
imperō	I order
exspectās	you wait for
Administrat	he, she, *or* it manages
demonstrāmus	we show

C) Translate these words from the first seven weeks. Listed at the bottom are the week in which the words were given.

amō	I love	liber	book
ēt	and	magnus	large
laudō	I praise	ōs	mouth
audiō	I hear	līberō	I set free
domus	house *or* home	fēmina	woman
flūmen	river	silva	forest
nihil	nothing	faciō	I make *or* do
exspectō	I wait for	dēspērō	I despair of
head	*caput*	*good*	*bonus*
moon	*luna*	*body*	*corpus*

amō, *head,* et (Week 1); laudō, audiō, domus (Week 2); *moon,* flūmen, nihil (Week 3); liber, *good,* magnus (Week 4); ōs, līberō, *body* (Week 5); fēmina, silva, faciō (Week 6); dēspērō, exspectō (Week 7).

D) Translate the following Latin quotations to English:

- "Cave canem": Beware of the dog

- "et cetera": and the rest

- "Dum spiro, spero" While I breathe, I hope

- "Dirigo": I direct

- "Semper fidelis": Always faithful

- "In principio creavit Deus caelum et terram": In the beginning God created the heavens and the earth.

E) List a derivative for each of the following words:

audiō	auditorium, audit	mater	maternal, maternity
sol	solar, solstice	terra	terrestrial
portō	portable, import	liber	library

F) Write the chants in the following boxes:

amō	amāmus
amās	amātis
amat	amant

sum	sumus
es	estis
est	sunt

ō	mus
s	tis
t	nt

bō	bimus
bis	bitis
bit	bunt

bam	bāmus
bās	bātis
bat	bant

Weekly Worksheet 8

A) In the boxes, conjugate the verbs from this week that change as "video" does. Translate the first two verbs in the boxes on the right.

moveō	movēmus		I move	we move
movēs	movētis		you move	you (all) move
movet	movent		he, she, it moves	they move

sedeō	sedēmus		I sit	we sit
sedēs	sedētis		you sit	you (all) sit
sedet	sedent		he, she, it sits	they sit

valeō	valēmus		I am well	we are well
valēs	valētis		you are well	you (all) are well
valet	valent		he, she, it is well	they are well

- Verbs that conjugate like "videō" are in the "e" family (or) second conjugation.

How do you know which family this verb belongs to? The other verb for this week changes like "amō." Conjugate it in the box below.

navigō	navigāmus
navigās	navigātis
navigat	navigant

- "Amō" and "navigo" are in the "a" family (or) <u>first</u> conjugation.

B) Try to give a derivative from memory for each of the following words:

patria	patriotic, patriot	aqua	aquarium, aquatic
navis	navy, naval	moveō	move
navigō	navigate	nox	nocturnal

C) Write two sentences in English. In each sentence, replace two of the words with Latin words from this week. One sentence is given as an example.

1. The *evening star* is shining in the *night.*   The *vesper* is shining in the *nox*

2. *Aqua* rushed downstream past the *navis.*

3. The happy *nauta* sees his *patria.*

D) What does "ex libris" mean? <u>from the books</u>

Where might you find that phrase used? <u>on the inside cover of a book</u>

E) Write and translate the chant for this week (pg. 17).

videō	vidēmus	I see	we see
vidēs	vidētis	you see	you (all) see
videt	vident	he, she, it sees	they see

F) Translate these words from earlier weeks.

mater	mother	cogitō	I think
dō	I give	lux	light
doceō	I teach	parvus	little
mūtō	I change	pēs	foot
faciō	I make *or* do	nomen	name

Weekly Worksheet 9

A) Conjugate and translate this 2nd-conjugation verb from the "e" family.

timeō	timēmus	I fear	we fear
timēs	timētis	you fear	you (all) fear
timet	timent	he, she, it fears	they fear

B) Translate these words from this week's word list on page 18.

oppugnō	I attack	capiō	I take *or* capture
metus	fear	perīculum	danger
castellum	castle	contra	against
fire	*ignis*	*sword*	*gladius*

C) Fill in the blank by deciding what Latin word the English word comes from. Then choose and underline the correct definition of the English word, by thinking about the Latin word.

1. *Equestrian* comes from <u>equus</u>. In an *equestrian* competition, people would:

    a) shoot with bows and arrows

    b) bake cakes and cookies

    c) <u>ride horses</u>

2. *Timid* is derived from <u>timeō</u> . *Timid* means:

    a) <u>fearful</u>

    b) bold

    c) talkative

3.   *Military* is a derivative of <u>mīles</u>. A *military* uniform is worn by a:

    a) nurse

    b) bus driver

    c) <u>soldier</u>

4.   *Terrify* comes from <u>terrēo</u>. A *terrifying* movie is:

    a) funny

    b) <u>very frightening</u>

    c) sad

5.   *Invincible* is a derivative of <u>vincō</u>. If a kingdom is *invincible,* it can't be:

    a) attacked

    b) <u>conquered</u>

    c) seen

D. Translate "ante bellum": <u>before the war</u> (In the United States, when we use this phrase we mean before the Civil <u>War</u>.)

E. Write this week's chant in the box. Do you recognize the pattern from a previous chant?

possum	possumus
potes	potestis
potest	possunt

F. Draw all of these things in a picture and label them. (A drawing page is provided on page 128.)

mīles	equus	nauta	castellum	navis
arbor	silva	collis	insula	avis
sol	flūmen	mare	mons	domus

Weekly Worksheet 10

A) Conjugate and translate the verbs in the boxes.

<u>Second</u> conjugation (or) "<u>e</u>" family

debeō	debēmus
debēs	debētis
debet	debent

I owe *or* ought	we owe
you owe	you (all) owe
he, she, it owes	they owe

<u>First</u> conjugation (or) "<u>a</u>" family

servō	servāmus
servās	servātis
servat	servant

I save	we save
you save	you (all) save
he, she, it saves	they save

B) Underline the endings of these verbs and then translate them.

navigā<u>mus</u>	we sail	sede<u>ō</u>	I sit
vale<u>t</u>	he is well	habē<u>s</u>	you have
move<u>nt</u>	they move	terre<u>nt</u>	they fear
timē<u>tis</u>	you (all) fear	oppugna<u>t</u>	he attacks
serva<u>t</u>	he saves	dēbē<u>mus</u>	we owe *or* ought

C) Translate the vocabulary from this week's word list on page 19.

familia	household	*fame, glory*	glōria
fīlia	daughter	crux	cross
lex	law	rēx	king

nunc	now	vīta	life
servō	I save	fīlius	son
precor	I pray	agō	I do *or* act
homō	man, human being	regō	I rule
I owe *or* ought	dēbēo		

D) Give two derivatives for each of these words.

	Derivitave	Derivitave
lex	legal, legislature, illegal, legislative, legitimate	
rēx	regal, regalia, regicide, royal	
vīta	vitamin, vital, vitality	

E) Write the chant for this week (pg. 19).

a	ae
ae	ārum
ae	īs
am	ās
āae	īs

- Provide this week's quotation (P.S.) and its translation.
  post scriptum = written afterwards

Weekly Worksheet 11

A) On the following lines, count to ten in Latin.

(1) one	(2) two	(3) three	(4) four	(5) five
ūnus	duo	trēs	quattor	quinque

(6) six	(7) seven	(8) eight	(9) nine	(10) ten
sex	septem	octō	novem	decem

B) There are many derivatives of this week's words in English. Answer these questions about some of them.

1. How many years are there in a *decade*? <u>ten</u>

2. How many years are there in a *millennium*? <u>a thousand</u>

3. How old is a state when it has a *centennial* celebration? <u>a hundred years</u>

4. How many musicians perform a *duet*? <u>two</u>

5. How many singers are in a *quartet*? <u>four</u>

6. How many babies are there when *quintuplets* are born? <u>five</u>

7. How many sides does an *octagon* have? <u>eight</u>

8. How many couples dance in a *quadrille*? <u>four</u>

9. In the Roman calendar, what "number" was the month of *September*? <u>the seventh</u>

10. How many horns does a *unicorn* have? How many wheels does a *unicycle* have? <u>one</u>

11. What Latin number do *union, unite,* and *uniform* come from? <u>ūnus</u>

C) The motto of the United States is "e pluribus unum." What does that mean?

<u>one out of many</u>

What is "e" an abbreviation for? (It's a word you've learned.) <u>ex</u>

D) Write the chant (pg. 20).

us	ī
ī	ōrum
ō	īs
um	ōs
ō	īs

Weekly Worksheet 12

A) Conjugate and translate the verbs in the boxes.

stō	stāmus
stās	stātis
stat	stant

I stand	we stand
you stand	you (all) stand
he, she, it stands	they stand

audeō	audēmus
audēs	audētis
audet	audent

I dare	we dare
you dare	you (all) dare
he, she, it dares	they dare

- The verb *stō* is in <u>first</u> conjugation (or) "<u>a</u>" family.

- The verb *audeō* is in <u>second</u> conjugation (or) "<u>e</u>" family.

B) Translate these verbs and underline the endings.

dubitat	he, she, *or* it doubts	volant	they fly
servāmus	we save	timētis	you (all) fear
terrent	they frighten	oppugnās	you attack

C) Translate the following Latin sentences to English.

- Dominus servat.   <u>The Lord (or lord or master) saves.</u>
- Mīles audet.   <u>The soldier dares.</u>
- Avis volat.   <u>The bird flies.</u>
- Servis stat.   <u>The slave stands.</u>
- Servi stant.   <u>The slaves stand.</u>

D) Fill in the blanks about derivatives of this week's words.

- *Audacious* comes from the Latin word <u>audeō</u>. If someone is *audacious*, he is very <u>daring</u>.

- *Facile* is a derivative of <u>facilis</u>. A *facile* task is an <u>easy</u> task.

- *Mesa* comes from <u>mensa</u>. Why does that make sense?

  <u>A mesa is called a "tableland" because it has a flat top.</u>

E) Finish this chant.

ī	imus
istī	istis
it	ērunt

F) Quotation:

What does A.D. stand for in Latin? What is the English translation?

<u>Anno Domini—In the year of our Lord</u>

Weekly Worksheet 13

A) List the verbs from this week on the blank lines below:

teneō   pareō   moneō   <u>spectō</u>   doleō

- From the group of verbs above, <u>double underline</u> the verb in the first conjugation or "a" family. The rest of the verbs are all in the <u>second</u> conjugation or "<u>e</u>" family.

B) From memory, translate these words from Latin to English. Most of these words are from previous word lists.

digitus	finger	auris	ear
capillus	hair	faciēs	face
cor	heart	corpus	body
oculus	eye	crūs	leg
pēs	foot	ōs	mouth
bracchium	arm	manus	hand

- While the Latin word for *heart* is *cor*, the French word for it is *coeur*. What is the name of the lake in northern Idaho with *coeur* in its name? <u>Lake Coeur d' Alene</u>

C) Translate the following words from English to Latin and underline the verb endings.

I obey	pareō	*we look at*	spectāmus
He grieves	dolet	*they obey*	parent
mind	mens	*strong*	fortis
sweet	dulcis	*thank you!*	gratiās agō

D) Write the chant for this week (pg. 22).

erō	erimus
eris	eritis
erit	erint

E) Quotation:
"Gloria in excelsis Deo." What does it mean? <u>Glory to God in the highest</u>

F) This is from the Latin Bible. See if you can figure out what it says.

<u>et</u> subito facta est cum angelo multitudo <u>militiae</u> <u>caelestis</u> <u>laudantium</u>
<u>Deum</u> <u>et</u> dicentium <u>gloria</u> <u>in</u> altissimis Deo <u>et</u> <u>in</u> <u>terra</u> pax <u>in</u> hominibus
bonae voluntatis.

<u>and suddenly there was with the angel a multitude of the heavenly host praising</u>
<u>God and saying Glory to God in the highest and on earth peace to men of good</u>
<u>will.</u>

Weekly Worksheet 14
(Test Practice / Weeks 8–14)

A) Conjugate each verb according to its conjugation or family.

occupō	occupāmus
occupās	occupātis
occupat	occupant

moveō	movēmus
movēs	movētis
movet	movent

dēbeō	dēbēmus
dēbēs	dēbētis
dēbet	dēbent

sedeō	sedēmus
sedēs	sedētis
sedet	sedent

B) Translate these verbs and underline the verb endings.

dēbēs	you owe *or* ought	habēmus	we have
paret	he, she, *or* it obeys	necant	they kill
respondētis	you (all) answer	doleō	I grieve
audent	they dare	flēmus	we weep
timēs	you fear	terret	he, she, it frightens
statīs	you (all) stand	doceō	I teach
he saves	*servat*	*they destroy*	*dēlēnt*
it flies	*volat*	*we warn*	*monēmus*

C) Translate these words from the last seven weeks.

patria	native land	navis	ship
diēs	day	*sailor*	*nauta*
war	*bellum*	cōpiae	troops
vīta	life	nunc	now
king	*rēx*	mille	a thousand
dominus	lord *or* master	porta	door *or* gate
slave	*servus*	*mind*	*mens*
cor	heart	auris	ear

---

patria, navis, diēs, *sailor* (Week 8); *war,* cōpiae (Week 9); vīta, nunc, *king* (Week 10); mille (Week 11); dominus, porta, *slave* (Week 12); *mind,* cor, auris (Week 13)

D) Use your knowledge of Latin quotations to answer these questions.

• An *ante-bellum* mansion was built before the war.

• "Ex libris John" in a book tells you it is from the books of John.

• *A.D. 70* stands for Anno Domini 70 and translated it is: .In the year of our Lord 70.

- When you see *p.s.* at the end of a letter, it stands for <u>post scriptum</u> which is translated <u>written afterwards</u>.
- "e pluribus unum" on a penny is translated <u>one out of many</u>.
- When you sing "Gloria in excelsis Deo," what are you singing? <u>Glory to God in the highest.</u>

E) Give a derivative for each of these words.

mens	mental	spectō	spectator, spectacles
nauta	nautical	nox	nocturnal
mīles	military, militia	vīta	vitamin, vitality, vital

F) Count from one to ten in Latin.

(1) one	(2) two	(3) three	(4) four	(5) five
ūnus	duo	trēs	quattor	quinque

(6) six	(7) seven	(8) eight	(9) nine	(10) ten
sex	septem	octō	novem	decem

G) Write the chants in the boxes from memory.

videō	vidēmus
vidēs	vidētis
videt	vident

possum	possumus
potes	potestis
potest	possunt

Write the chants in the boxes from memory (continued from "G" on last page).

a	ae
ae	ārum
ae	īs
aam	ās
ā	īs

us	ī
ī	ōrum
ō	īs
um	ōs
ō	īs

ī	imus
istī	istis
it	ērunt

erō	erimus
eris	eritis
erit	erint

Weekly Worksheet 15

A) Write the chant for this week in the box (pg. 24).

eram	erāmus
erās	erātis
erat	erant

B) List the verbs for this week according to whether they are of the first or second conjugation. Hint: There are two words in the first conjugation or "a" family, and three words in the second conjugation or "e" family. You will have some blanks in each of the columns. Fill the spaces with verbs you've learned that belong to each conjugation.

First Conjugation	Second Conjugation
iuvō	augeō
communicō	mereō
*amō	maneō
*laudō	*terreō
*servō	*videō

C) Conjugate the following verbs in the boxes below.

First Conjugation (or) "a" Family

iuvō	iuvāmus
iuvās	iuvātis
iuvat	iuvant

Second Conjugation (or) "e" Family

augeo	augēmus
augēs	augētis
auget	augent

D) The words in italics in the sentences below are derivatives of words from this week. Underline the correct choice based on the Latin words you've learned.

- *Urban* planning is planning of:

  gardens   parties   <u>cities</u>

- An *edifice* is a large:

  <u>building</u>   forest   arena

- If a ship is sailing to New York *via* the Panama Canal, it is:

  Avoiding the canal   <u>Going by way of the canal</u>   Not really going

E) Give this week's quotation and its translation (pg. 24).

<u>"cum laude"—with praise</u>

Weekly Worksheet 16

A) Write the chant for this week (pg. 25).

r	mur
ris	minī
tur	ntur

B) Decline the following nouns:

Second Declension (or) "e" Family

mūrus	mūrī
mūrī	mūrōrum
mūrō	mūrīs
murum	murōs
mūrō	mūrīs

First Declension (or) "a" Family

praeda	praedae
praedae	praedārum
praedae	praedīs
praedam	praedās
praedā	praedīs

- What declension is "mūrus"? <u>Second</u> "Praeda" is in the <u>first</u> declension.

C) Conjugate the following verbs:

First Conjugation (or) "a" Family

putō	putāmus
putās	putātis
putat	putant

First Conjugation (or) "a" Family

parō	parāmus
parās	parātis
parat	parant

D) Translate the following verbs and underline the endings.

recuperā<u>mus</u>	we recover, recuperate	exerce<u>ō</u>	I train *or* exercise
superā<u>tis</u>	you (all) conquer	timē<u>s</u>	you fear
he thinks	*puta<u>t</u>*	*they prepare*	*paran<u>t</u>*

E) Give the Latin word that each of these English words is derived from. Use the word list on page 25.

mural	mūrus	recuperate	recuperō
vulnerable	vulnus	campus	campus
prince, principal	princeps		

F) Translate this Latin quotation and describe the story behind it:

"Hannibal ad portas"—Hannibal is at the gates

(This quotation is discussed on the video. If you don't have access to the video, look for an account of Hannibal's battles at Ticinus River, Trebbia River, Lake Trasimenus, and Cannae, and his pursuit of victory in Rome.)

Weekly Worksheet 17

A) Complete the definition of a noun.
    A noun <u>names a person, place, or thing.</u>

- Translate these words and <u>double-underline</u> the nouns.

    nuntius   <u>__messenger__</u>   exercitus   <u>__training _or_ exercise__</u>

    perturbō   <u>I confuse</u>   lēgātus   <u>__lieutenant__</u>

- This is more difficult. Is "pugna" a noun or a verb? <u>Noun</u>
    Example:
        In one of these sentences, "fight" is a noun, and in the other it is a verb.
        Underline the sentence where "fight" is the used like "pugna."

    ⬭ The fight was fierce. ⬭   The armies will fight tomorrow.

B) Use a dictionary and write the definition of these English words on the lines below. In the parentheses, write the Latin words from which each word is derived.

    hostile: having to do with an enemy; feeling or showing hatred
    _____   (hostis   )

    antique: of or belonging to ancient times; made in an earlier period
    _____   (antīquus   )

    famous: generally recorded in history or currently known
    _____   (fāma   )

C) Write the chant for this week (pg. 26).

bor	bimur
beris	biminī
bitur	**buntur**

D) What is the English translation for "terra incognita"? <u>Unknown land</u>

Weekly Worksheet 18

A) Draw lines to match the Latin words on the left with their English derivatives on the right.

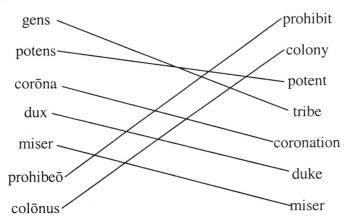

gens   prohibit

potens   colony

corōna   potent

dux   tribe

miser   coronation

prohibeō   duke

colōnus   miser

B) Write the chant for this week (pg. 27).

bār	bāmur
bāris	bāminī
bātur	bāntur

C) First underline the verb endings then translate these sentences.

* Rēgīna probat. <u>The queen approves.</u>

* Rēgīna non probat.   <u>The queen does not approve.</u>

* Dux recusat.   <u>The leader refuses.</u>

* Dux non recusat.   <u>The leader is not refusing.</u>

* Socii recusant <u>The partners refuse.</u>

D) Give the quotation for this week and its translation.

<u>"Veni, vidi, vici"—I came, I saw, I conquered</u>

Weekly Worksheet 19

A) Use what you know about these derivatives to complete the sentences.

- A *spelunker* is someone who explores   <u>caves</u>.

- A person with an *aquiline* nose has a nose like an   <u>eagle</u>.

- If you are *satisfied*, you've had   <u>enough</u>.

B) Translate the following words from English to Latin using the word list on page 28.

breeze	aura	bull	taurus
eagle	aquila	bank	ripa
cloud	nimbus	plant	herba
caves	spēlunca	wolf	lupus

C) Provide the Latin for these plural nouns according to their declension or family. See page 19 for First Declension (or) "a" family and page 20 for Second Declension (or) "us" family.

breezes	aurae	bulls	taurī
eagles	aquilae	banks	ripae
clouds	nimbī	plants	herbae
caves	spēluncae	wolves	lupī

D) First underline the pronouns, then translate the verbs from English to Latin. Hint: What verb ending do these words share?

it flourishes	florēt	she finds out	explōrat
he hides	occultat	he delights	dēlectat
he approves	probat	she refuses	recusat
it confuses	perturbat	it harms	nocet
she prepares	parat	he thinks	cogitat *or* putat

E) Who said "et tu, Brute" and what does it mean?

<u>Julius Caesar said it to Brutus as he was stabbed. It means "even you, Brutus."</u>
<u>A more detailed explanation appears on the Video Tape.</u>

F) In the space below, draw a map of Italy. Label the city of Rome and also the Alps. (A drawing page is provided on pg. 129.)

Weekly Worksheet 20

A) Write the chant for this week in the box (pg. 29).

Second Declension (Neuter)

Singular	Plural
um	a
ī	ōrum
ō	īs
um	a
ō	īs

Second Decl. Chant

Singular	Plural
us	ī
ī	ōrum
ō	īs
um	ōs
ō	īs

B) Translate the following nouns into Latin from the work list on page 29. Use Second Declension Neuter endings. Notice that some of the words are plural.

words	verba	rocks	saxa
gift	dōnum	shield	scūtum
kindness	beneficia	rewards	praemia
kingdom	regnum	leaf	folium

C) Underline the noun that goes with the verb and then translate the sentences.

Noun	Verb	
• Dōnum / Dōna.	delectant	The gifts delight.
• Signum / Signa	perturbant.	The signs confuse.
• Regnum / Regna	auget.	The kingdom increases.
• Tēlum / Tēla	nocet.	The weapon harms.

D) Choose three of these words to look up in an English dictionary. Write down the definition on the lines. In the parentheses, write the Latin word from which each word is derived.

foliage	beneficial	premium	stagnant
pabulum	regnant	verb	

foliage:	The leaves of growing plants.	(folium)
beneficial:	Helpful in the meeting of needs.	(beneficium)
pabulum	Something that nourishes; food.	(pābulum)
regnant:	Reigning; ruling. Predominant. Widespread.	(regnum)
premium	A prize or bonus given as inducement.	(praemium)
stagnant	Not moving or flowing. Motionless.	(stagnum)
verb	A member of a class of words; expressing action.	(verbum)

E) Translate the following Second Declension Neuter nouns ending in *um*. (All the words are in the word lists from previous weeks.)

caelum	sky	bracchium	arm
oppidum	town	aedificium	building
perīculum	danger	bellum	war
castellum	castle	sōlum	floor

F) What does "excelsior" mean? Of what state is it the motto?

Ever upward—New York

Weekly Worksheet 21

A) In boxes, write the endings for the following declensions:

First declension	
Singular	Plural
a	ae
ae	ārum
ae	īs
am	ās
ā	īs

Second declension	
Singular	Plural
us	ī
ī	ōrum
ō	īs
um	ōs
ō	īs

Second decl. (neuter)	
Singular	Plural
um	a
ī	ōrum
ō	īs
um	a
ō	īs

B) Translate the following nouns into Latin. When you use an ending, underline it in the boxes above, only using the nominative case.

charioteers	aurīgae	twin	geminus
word	verbum	leaves	folia
dawn	aurōra	male bears	ursī

C) Give the singular and plural forms of these nouns in Latin.

	Singular	Plural
water carrier	aquārius	aquāriī
archer	sagittārius	sagittāriī
scorpion	scorpius	scorpiī
messenger	nuntius	nuntiī
son	fīlius	fīliī

D) Answer the following questions about derivatives on this week's "extra credit" words list.

- What country got its name from the Latin word for "southern"? <u>Australia</u>

- Look at your word list. What is another name for Northern Lights, based on two words from the list? <u>Aurora Borealis</u>

E) Translate the following sentences.

- *The lion* frightens.　　*<u>Leō terret.</u>*

- *The maiden* praises.　　*<u>Virgō laudat.</u>*

- Scorpius nocet.　　<u>The scorpion harms.</u>

- *The bears increase.*　　*<u>Ursi (or ursae) augent.</u>*

- *The twins* grieve.　　*<u>Gemini dolent.</u>*

- Piscis volat.　　<u>The fish flies.</u>

Weekly Worksheet 22

A) Complete the following chants.

amō	amāmus		videō	vidēmus
amās	amātis		vidēs	vidētis
amat	amant		videt	vident

- *Amō* is in the <u>first</u> conjugation (or) "<u>a</u>" family.
- *Videō* is in the <u>second</u> conjugation (or) "<u>e</u>" family.

B) Conjugate the following verbs.

placeō	placēmus		errō	errāmus
placēs	placētis		errās	errātis
placet	placent		errat	errant

- *Placeō* is in the <u>second</u> conjugation (or) "<u>e</u>" family.
- *Errō* is in the <u>first</u> conjugation (or) "<u>a</u>" family.

C) Translate these verbs and underline the endings.

rogātis	you (all) ask	recitāmus	we read aloud
appellant	they name	placet	he, she, or it pleases
I read aloud	*recitō*	*you wander*	*errās*

D) Translate "Cogito ergo sum." <u>I think, therefore I am</u>. Now translate the following sentences containing *sum* or other forms of the *sum* chant.

- Contentus sum.   I am content. (male/boy)

- Beāta sum.   I am happy. (or blessed) (female/girl)

- Beātus es.   You are blessed. (or happy) (male/boy)

- Honestus est.   He is honorable. (male/boy)

- Improbus est.   He is wicked. (male/boy)

E) Fill in the missing words in this week's chant (pg. 31).

hic	haec	hoc
huius	huius	huius
huic	huic	huic
hunc	hanc	hoc
hōc	hāc	hōc

Weekly Worksheet 23

A) Write the rest of this chant in the box.

hī	hae	haec
hōrum	hārum	hōrum
hīs	hīs	hīs
hōs	hās	haec
hīs	hīs	hīs

B) Translate these sentences.

1. Ventus auget.	The wind increases.
2. Tempestās mūtat.	The weather changes.
3. Undae sunt magnae.	The waves are big.
4. Classis errat.	The fleet wanders.
5. Nautae clamant et laborant.	The sailors shout and work.
6. Mare non est aequum.	The seas is not calm.
7. Ancora non movebit.	The anchor will not move.
8. Piscis nat	The fish swims.

C) Underline the correct meaning of these derivatives.

- An *itinerary* is

    a) a menu   b) a lengthy letter   c) the route of a journey

- An *itinerant* preacher

    a) cannot read   b) travels from place to place   c) is quiet

- If a field of grass is *undulating*, it is

    a) parched from drought   b) flourishing   c) <u>waving in the wind</u>

- A *tempest* is a

    a) <u>violent rainstorm</u>   b) lacy curtain   c) high riverbank

D) "Deo Volente" is sometimes abbreviated "D.V." It means <u>God willing</u>.

E) Draw a picture with these things in it: ancora, nauta, remus, ora, unda, tempestas, navis, classis, portus, saxum. Label them. (A blank page is provided on pg. 130.)

Weekly Worksheet 24

A) Write this week's chant in the boxes (pg. 33).

ego	nōs
mei	nostrum
mihi	nōbīs
mē	nōs
mē	nōbīs

tū	vōs
tuī	vestrum
tibi	vōbīs
tē	vōs
tē	vōbīs

B) Give the singular and plural forms of these nouns in Latin.

	Singular	Plural
penalty	poena	poenae
church	ecclēsia	ecclēsiae
apostle	apostolus	apostoli

First declension

Singular	Plural
a	ae
ae	ārum
ae	īs
am	ās
ā	īs

Second declension

Singular	Plural
us	ī
ī	ōrum
ō	īs
um	ōs
ō	īs

C) Translate these words from the list on page 33 to English and indicate whether each is a noun, verb, or adjective (part of speech).

	Translation	Part of Speech
vērus, a, um	true	adjective
crēdō	I believe	verb
praedicō	I proclaim	verb
fidēs	faith	noun
vīvus, a, um	living	adjective

D) Conjugate *praedicō*. In addition, label the columns singular or plural and indicate first, second, or third person.

First–Second–Third	(Singular)	(Plural)
First	praedicō	praedicāmus
Second	praedicās	praedicātis
Third	praedicat	praedicant

E) Translate this: "Iesus, Rex Iudaeorum." <u>Jesus, King of the Jews.</u>

Weekly Worksheet 25

A) Sort the following words into four lists: people, places people live, animals, and places animals live.

ager, agricola, rēgīna, lupus, urbs, cīvis, ursa, equus, castellum, mare, domus, mater, spēlunca, stabulum, piscis, silva, villa, avis, nauta, navis

People

1. rēgīna
2. mater
3. agricola
4. cīvis
5. nauta

Places People Live

1. castellum
2. domus
3. villa
4. urbs
5. navis

Animals

1. ursa
2. equus
3. piscis
4. lupus
5. avis

Places Animals Live

1. spēlunca
2. stabulum
3. mare
4. silva
5. ager

B) There are three words from this week's list which have English derivatives that are spelled exactly in each language. List them.

1. villa   2. animal   3. pastor

C) Conjugate "vulnerō" in the present tense.

vulnerō	vulnerāmus
vulnerās	vulnerātis
vulnerat	vulnerant

D) Translate "Sic Semper Tyrannis." <u>Thus always to tyrants.</u>
This is the motto for the state of Virginia.

Weekly Worksheet 26

A) Conjugate cen
seō in the present tense.

This verb is in the <u>Second</u> Conjugation (or) the "<u>e</u>" family.

censeō	censēmus
censēs	censētis
censet	censent

B) Translate these verbs and underline the endings.

vītā<u>mus</u>   we avoid   vīta<u>nt</u>   they avoid

postulabī<u>mus</u>   we will demand   postula<u>t</u>   he, she, or it demands

cense<u>bunt</u>   they will estimate   censē<u>tis</u>   you (all) estimate

C) Translate these sentences.

1. Agricola censet.	The farmer estimates.
2. Adulēscēns vītat.	The young man avoids.
3. Civis postulabit.	The citizen will demand.

D) Underline the meaning of these derivatives of this week's words on page 35.

- If something is *mediocre*, it is:

a) very interesting   b) <u>neither good or bad</u>   c) bright

- *Linguistics* is:

  a) the study of rain   b) an Italian food   c) <u>the science of language</u>

- If a danger is *inevitable*, it can't:

  a) be seen   b) <u>be avoided</u>   c) be overcome

E) Translate "In hoc signo vinces." In this sign you will conquer.

Weekly Worksheet 27

A) Fill in these blanks about derivatives of words from this week's list on page 36.

- *Annual* comes from the Latin word <u>annus</u>. If something happens *annually*, it happens every <u>year.</u>

- *Multitude* is a derivative of <u>multus</u>. When Jesus talked to the *multitudes*, he was talking to <u>many</u> people.

- *Procrastinate* is derived from <u>crās</u>. It means <u>put off something until tomorrow.</u>

B) Translate these sentences, label the Subject Noun (SN) and Verb (V) in each sentence, and underline the endings on the verbs.

1. Avus recitat.	The grandfather reads aloud.
2. Adulēscēns rogabit.	The young man will ask.
3. Ecclesia crēdat.	The church believes.
4. Tempus volat.	Time flies.

(Another way of saying this is *tempus fugit*.)

C) Quotation. Give the unabbreviated Latin and then the translation of these:

	Latin	Translation
a.m.	ante meridiem	before noon
p.m.	post meridiem	after noon
A.D.	Anno Domini	In the year of our lord
P.S.	post scriptem	written afterwards

- What does "ante-bellum" mean? <u>before the war</u>

- The Vulgate is a Latin translation of the Bible. In the book of John, when Pilate brings Jesus out before the people, Pilate says *"Ecce homō!"* What does this mean?

  <u>Behold the man!</u>

fīnis!

TRANSLATION TOOLS

NUMBER CHART

LATIN	ITALIAN	SPANISH	FRENCH
ūnus	un(o)	un(o)	un
duo	due	dos	deux
trēs	tre	tres	trois
quattuor	quattro	cuatro	quatre
quīnque	cinque	cinco	cinq
sex	sei	seis	six
septem	sette	siete	sept
octō	otto	ocho	huit
novem	nove	nueve	Neuf
decem	dieci	diez	dix
ūndecim	undici	once	onze
duodecim	dodici	doce	douze
centum	cento	ciento	cent
mīlle	mille	mil	mille

LATIN STATE MOTTOES

1. Ad astra per aspera—"To the stars through difficulties" (Kansas)

2. Alias volat propriis—"She flies on her own wings" (Oregon)

3. Animis opibusque parati—"Prepared in minds and resources" (South Carolina)

4. Audemus jura nostra defendere—"We dare to defend our rights" (Alabama)

5. Crescit eundo—"It grows as it goes" (New Mexico)

6. Dirigo—"I direct" (Maine)

7. Ditat Deus—"God enriches" (Arizona)

8. Dum spiro, spero—"While I breathe, I hope" (South Carolina)*

9. Ense petit placidam sub libertate quietem—" By the sword we seek peace, but peace only under liberty" (Massachusetts)

10. Esse quam videri—"To be rather than to seem" (North Carolina)

11. Esto perpetua—"May she be forever" (Idaho)

12. Excelsior—"Ever upward" (New York)

13. Labor omnia vincit—"Labor conquers all things"

14. Montani semper liberi—"Mountaineers are always freemen" (West Virginia)

15. Nil sine numine— "Nothing without providence" (Colorado)

16. Qui transtulit sustinet—"He who transplanted still sustains" (Connecticut)

17. Regnat populus—"The people rule" (Arkansas)

18. Salus populi suprema lex esto—"The welfare of the people shall be the supreme law" (Missouri)

19. Si quaeris peninsulam amoenam, circumspice—"If you seek a pleasant peninsula, look about you" (Michigan)

20. Sic semper tyrannis—"Thus always to tyrants" (Virginia)

21. Virtute et armis—"By valor and arms" (Mississippi)

22. Sicut patribus, sit Deus nobis—"As with our fathers, may God be with us" (Boston)

* South Carolina has two state motto's.

CONSTELLATIONS

Andromeda	Antlia	Apus	Aquarius	Aquila
Ara	Aries	Auriga	Boötes	Caelum
Camelopardalis	Cancer	Canes Venatici	Canis Major	Canis Minor
Capricornus	Carina	Cassiopeia	Centaurus	Cepheus
Cetus	Chameleon	Circinus	Columba	Coma Berenices
Corona Austrina	Corona Borealis	Corvus	Crater	Crux
Cygnus	Delphinus	Dorado	Draco	Equuleus
Eridanus	Fornax	Gemini	Grus	Hercules
Horologium	Hydra	Hydrus	Indus	Lacerta
Leo	Leo Minor	Lepus	Libra	Lupus
Lynx	Lyra	Mensa	Microscopium	Monoceros
Musca	Norma	Octans	Ophiuchus	Orion
Pavo	Pegasus	Perseus	Phoenix	Pictor
Pisces	Piscis Austrinus	Puppis	Pyxis	Reticulum
Sagitta	Sagittarius	Scorpius	Sculptor	Scutum
Serpens	Sextans	Taurus	Telescopium	Triangulum
Triangulum Australe	Tucana	Ursa Major	Ursa Minor	Vela
Virgo	Volans	Vulpecula		

WEEKLY QUOTATIONS

Each week, with a few exceptions, the students are expected to copy a quotation from the weekly word list to the weekly quotation page (beginning on page 115) and memorize it. Listed below are some of the better known or more useful Latin quotations. Included in the student book is a list of Latin state mottoes, some of which are included here.

Week	Latin Quote	English Translation
1	"et cetera"	and the rest
2	"Cave canem"	Beware of the dog
3	"In principio creavit Deus caelum et terram."	In the beginning God created the heavens and the earth.
4	"Semper fidelis"	always faithful
5	"dirigo"	I direct
6	"Dum spiro, spero"	While I breathe, I hope (South Carolina)
7	--	--
8	"ex libris"	from the books
9	"ante bellum"	before the war
10	"post scriptum"	written afterwards
11	"e pluribus unum"	one out of many
12	"Anno Domini"	In the year of our Lord
13	"Gloria in excelsis Deo"	Glory to God in the highest
14	--	--
15	"cum laude"	with praise
16	"Hannibal ad portas"	Hannibal is at the gates
17	"terra incognita"	unknown land
18	"Veni, vidi, vici"	I came, I saw, I conquered
19	"et tu, Brute"	Even you, Brutus
20	"excelsior"	ever higher (New York)
21	--	--
22	"Cogito ergo sum"	I think, therefore I am (Descartes)
23	"Deo volente"	God willing
24	"Iesus Rex Iudaeorum"	Jesus, King of the Jews
25	"Sic semper tyrannis"	Thus always to tyrants (Virginia)
26	"In hoc signo vinces"	In this sign you will conquer
27	"ante meridiem" / "post meridiem"	before noon / after noon

TEACHING TOOLS

PRONUNCIATION

Vowels:

Vowels in Latin have only two pronunciations, long and short. When speaking, long vowels are held twice as long as short vowels. Long vowels are marked with a "macron" or line over the vowel (e.g., ā). Vowels without a macron are short vowels.

When spelling a word, including the macron is important in order to determine the meaning of the word. (e.g., liber is a noun meaning *book*, and līber is an adjective meaning *free*.)

Long Vowels:

ā	like a in father:	frāter, suprā
ē	like e in obey:	trēs, rēgīna
ī	like i in machine	mīles, vīta
ō	like o in holy:	sōl, glōria
ū	like oo in rude:	flūmen, lūdus

Short Vowels:

a	like a in idea	canis, mare
e	like e in bet	et, terra
i	like i in this	hic, silva
o	like o in domain	bonus, nomen
u	like u in put	sum, sub

Diphthongs:

A combination of two vowel sounds collapsed together into one syllable:

ae	like ai in aisle	caelem, saepe
au	like ou in house	laudo, nauta
ei	like ei in reign	deinde
eu	like eew in Tuesday	Deus,
oe	like oi in oil	moenia, poena
ui	like ew in chewy	huius, hui

Consonants:

Latin consonants are pronounced with the same sounds with the following exceptions:

c	like c in come	never soft like city, cinema, or peace
g	like g in go	never soft like gem, geology, or gentle
v	like w in wow	never like vikings, victor, or vacation
s	like s in sissy	never like easel, weasel, or peas
ch	like ch in chorus	never like church, chapel, or children
r	is trilled	like a dog snarling, or a machine gun
i	like y in yes	when used before a vowel at the beginning of a word, between two vowels within a word, otherwise it's usually used as a vowel.

THE CHANT SHEET AND GENERAL GRAMMAR

The chant charts are listed in two different places in this book. First, you'll find the charts listed with the weekly word lists and quotations. Next, the chant charts are listed according to parts of speech (pg. 38) and chant order (pg. 41). Chants are one of the basic building blocks for the foundation of first year learning. Starting with *amo*, the students practice their chants together verbally each day. As new chants are learned, they are added to the recitation. The students need to have the chants memorized thoroughly and accurately by the end of this year; however, they don't need to fully understand how all the chants are used. Only those parts that need to be understood will be pointed out.

Conjugations:

A conjugation is a group of verbs (also known as a family of verbs), that change in the same way. To conjugate a verb means to list together, verbally or written, all of its forms. There are five different forms or characteristics of verbs: person, number, and tense, mood, and voice. The following is a brief discussion of the forms used:

- Person: Who is the subject? Who is doing the action?

  First Person: The speaker(s)—*I* or *we*
  Second Person: The person(s) spoken to—*you* or *you(all)*
  Third Person: The person(s) spoken about—*he, she, it,* or *they*

- Number: Is the subject single or plural? How many?

- Tense: When does the action take place? Latin has six tenses:

  Present System: (All formed on the present stem)
  Present: action right now.
  Future: action that will happen in the future.
  Imperfect: continuous or sustained action in the past.

  Perfect System: (All formed on a perfect, *active* or *passive*, stem)
  Perfect (present perfect): completed action in the past. (short-term)
  PluPerfect (past perfect): completed action prior to some time in the past.
  Future Perfect: completed action prior to some point in the future.

- Voice: A way to determine if the subject performs the action or receives it.

  Active Voice: The subject is peforming the action.
  Passive Voice: The subject is the receiver of the action.

- Mood: The method of expressing a verbal action or state of being.

  Indicative: Indicates "real" action that has, in fact, occurred.
  Imperative: Commands someone to take action not yet occurred.
  Subjunctive: Describes potential, hypothetical action to take place.

Stem:

A stem is the underlying base of a word, an unchanging part, a root, to which endings may be added to change the form of the word to indicate person, number, tense, voice, and mood.

Principal Parts:

In order to determine the perfect active stem of a Latin verb, you first have to know the principal parts of the verb. In some respects, the principal parts of an English verb are similar to the principal parts in Latin verbs. Most regular Latin verbs have four principal parts:

Present Active Indicative:	I praise, *laudō*
Present Active Infinitive	to praise, *laudāre*
Perfect Active Indicative	I praised, have praised, *laudāvī*
Perfect Passive Participle	praised, having been praised, *laudātum*

Verb Paradigms (Patterns)

On page 38, the first four chants listed, *amō, videō, sum* and *possum,* are complete verbs in the present tense.

In Latin, there are four different verb conjugations. Also, there are several irregular verbs which do not belong to a conjugation or family. The third and fourth conjugations will be introduced in later years. In this book, the following will be covered:

1. First conjugation—"a" family is represented by *amō.*
2. Second conjugation—"e" family is represented by *videō.*
3. Irregular Verbs—sum and possum.

- *Amō* (First conjugation or "a" family)

Any verb that is in the first conjugation or "a" family will follow the pattern that *amō* shows here. Notice that an "a" exists in the middle of every form except for the first person singular.

	Singular	Plural		Singular	Plural
1st	amō	amāmus	1st	laudō	laudāmus
2nd	amās	amātis	2nd	laudās	laudātis
3rd	amat	amant	3rd	laudat	laudant

In the box below, the stem of the Latin word dō is underlined. The stem is the unchanging part to which the endings that show person, number, and tense are added. Notice that an "a" exists in the middle of every form except for the first person singular. The same stem is used in the future and imperfect tenses, and the entire stem is there in all forms in those tenses.

	Singular	Plural
1st	dō	dāmus
2nd	dās	dātis
3rd	dat	dant

In the next year of Latin, the students will learn that the "a" comes from the infinitive form. In this year analysis is kept to a minimum by having them follow the *amō* paradigm for verbs that end in "o" and the *video* paradigm for verbs that end in "eō".

Included in the word lists for Latin Primer I is a small group of verbs where the "a"—"eō" rule will not work. Here are those words. (*Vīvō, dīrigō, scrībō, currō, vincō, agō, regō, volō, pōnō, crēdō, and serō* are in the third conjugation and therefore do not follow the pattern of *amō. Creō* is in the first conjugation although it looks like it would be in the second.) Verbs that end in "iō" such as *audiō, sciō, capiō,* and *faciō* are in the third or fourth conjugation. For now, simply teach the given form of third and fourth conjugation verbs and do not conjugate them.

• *Video* (Second conjugation or "e" family)

All verbs in the second conjugation or "e" family follow the example of *video.* The "e" at the end of the stem exists in all forms of the present, imperfect, and future tenses.

	Singular	Plural		Singular	Plural
1st	video	vidēmus	1st	doceō	docēmus
2nd	vidēs	vidētis	2nd	docēs	docētis
3rd	videt	vident	3rd	docet	docent

In the box below, the stem of the Latin word fleō is underlined. Notice that an "e" exists in the middle of every from except for the first person singular. The same stem is used in the future and imperfect tenses, and the entire stem is there in all forms in those tenses.

	Singular	Plural
1st	fleō	flēmus
2nd	flēs	flētis
3rd	flēt	flēnt

- *Sum*

Sum is the verb of "being" in the present tense. Like its counterpart in English, it is an irregular verb, although it does show considerable regularity in the endings of the forms. No endings are added onto sum. The translation of sum is shown in the box below. The meaning of the chant does not need to be learned as soon as the chant is memorized, but it should be learned thoroughly during the year.

	Singular	Plural
1st	sum	sumus
2nd	es	estis
3rd	est	sunt

	Singular	Plural
1st	I am	we are
2nd	you are	you(all) are
3rd	he, she it is	they are

- *Possum*

Possum means "I am able". Its forms are also irregular, with no added endings and not following any conjugation, but you can see that they are the forms of *sum* with "pot" or "pos" added at the beginning. If the corresponding form of *sum* begins with an "s", then "pos" is added; otherwise, "pot" is added.

	Singular	Plural
1st	possum	possumus
2nd	potes	potestis
3rd	potest	possunt

	Singular	Plural
1st	I am able	we are able
2nd	you are able	you(all) are able
3rd	he, she, it is able	they are able

The verb endings are listed on pages 38 and 39. The verb endings are added to stems to form complete verbs such as *amō* and *videō*. Although the students will only be translating the first two tenses during this year, you can see how all of these endings are used in the examples on the following pages. A first-conjugation verb, *laudō*, and a second-conjugation verb, *moveō*, are shown in each tense and translated. With the exception of the future tense endings, these endings are also used for the third and fourth conjugations of verbs. Notice the endings are in **bold**.

- Present Active Verb Ending (*ō, s, t)*

    An equally legitimate translation of the present tense is "I am praising," or "I do praise," "you are praising," or "you do praise," etc.

- Future Active Verb Ending (*bō, bis, bit)*

    Notice that the entire stem appears in every form in both conjugations, whether ending in "a" (first conjugation) or in "e" (second conjugation).

- Imperfect Active Verb Ending (*bam, bas, bat)*

    This is but one translation of the imperfect tense. The sense of it is an action that was ongoing in the past, so "I used to praise" or " I kept praising" would also translate *laudo*. It should not be translated as simple past since the <u>perfect tense</u> does that. The three tenses above have all used the present stem. A different stem will be used for the next three tenses.

- Perfect Active Verb Ending (*ī, isti, it)*

    There are two other translations of this tense: "I have praised" and "I did praise". The stem that is used here and will be used for the next two tenses is the perfect stem. In the first conjugation, the perfect stem for most verbs is the present stem + "v"; in the second conjugation there is less consistency.

- Future Perfect Active Verb Ending (*erō, eris, erit)*

- Pluperfect Active Verb Ending (*eram, eras, erat)*

    This tense derives its name from the Latin for "more than perfect" and designates action completed prior to a time in the past.

- Present Passive Verb Ending *(r, ris, tur)*

    This tense and the two that follow are in the passive voice, the subject of the verb receiving action rather than doing it. With one exception, this tense is formed by adding the endings to the present stem. The exception is in the first person singular form (*laudor* and *moneor)* where the ending is added to the full present tense active form. Also valid as a translation of the present passive is "I am being praised", etc.

- Future Passive Verb Ending (*bor, beris, bitur)*
    All of the endings are simply added to the present stem.

- Imperfect Passive Verb Ending (*bar, baris, batur)*

Verb Endings

Verb endings are added to verb stems to form complete verbs. A first conjugation or "a" family verb, *laudō*, and a second conjugation or "e" family verb, *moveō*, are shown in each tense and tranlated on the next two pages. The abbreviation (AV) represents "active voice" and (PV) represents "passive voice."

	Singular			Plural		
	1st	2nd	3rd	1st	2nd	3rd
Present (AV)	laudō	laudās	laudat	laudāmus	laudātis	laudant
Future (AV)	laudabō	laudābis	laudābit	laudābimus	laudābitis	laudābunt
Imperfect (AV)	laudābam	laudābas	laudābat	laudābāmus	laudābātis	laudābant
Perfect (AV)	laudāvi	laudāvisti	laudāvit	laudāvimus	laudāvistis	laudavērunt
Future Perfect (AV)	laudāvero	laudāveris	laudāverit	laudāverimus	laudāveritis	laudāverint
Pluperfect (AV)	laudāveram	laudāverās	laudāverat	laudāverāmus	laudāverātis	laudāverant
Present (PV)	laudor	laudāris	laudātur	laudāmur	laudāminī	laudāntur
Future (PV)	laudābor	laudāberis	laudābitur	laudābimur	laudābiminī	laudābuntur
Imperfect (PV)	laudābar	laudābāris	laudābātur	laudābāmur	laudābāmini	laudābantur

	Singular			Plural		
	1st	2nd	3rd	1st	2nd	3rd
Present (AV)	moveō	movēs	movet	movēmus	movētis	movent
Future (AV)	movebō	movebis	movebit	movebimus	movebitis	movebunt
Imperfect (AV)	movebam	movebas	movebat	movebāmus	movebātis	movebant
Perfect (AV)	movevi	movevisti	movevit	movevimus	movevistis	movērunt
Future Perfect (AV)	movero	moveris	moverit	moverimus	moveritis	moverint
Pluperfect (AV)	moveram	moverās	moverat	moverāmus	moverātis	moverant
Present (PV)	moveor	moveris	movetur	movemur	moveminī	moventur
Future (PV)	movebor	moveberis	movebitur	movebimur	movebiminī	movebuntu
Imperfect (PV)	movebar	movebāris	movebātur	movebāmur	movebāmini	movebantur

	Singular	Plural
	1st 2nd 3rd	1st 2nd 3rd
Present (AV)	I praise; you praise; he, she, or it praises	we praise; you (all) praise; they praise
Future (AV)	I shall praise; you will praise; he, she, or it will praise	we shall praise; you (all) will praise; they will praise
Imperfect (AV)	I was praising, you were praising; he, she, or it was praising	we were praising; you (all) were praising; they were praising
Perfect (AV)	I praised; you praised; he, she, or it praised	we praised; you (all) praised; they praised
Future Perfect (AV)	I shall have praised, you will have praised; he, she, or it will have praised	we shall have praised; you (all) will have praised; they will have praised
Pluperfect (AV)	I had praised; you had praised; he, she, or it had praised	we had praised; you (all) had praised; they had praised
Present (PV)	I am praised; you are praised; he, she, or it is praised	we are praised; you (all) are praised; they are praised
Future (PV)	I shall be praised; you will be praised; he, she, or it will be praised	we shall be praised; you (all) will be praised; they will be praised
Imperfect (PV)	I was being praised; you were being praised; he, she, or it was being praised	we were being praised; you (all) were being praised; they were being praised

	Singular	Plural
	1st 2nd 3rd	1st 2nd 3rd
Present (AV)	I move; you move; he, she, or it moves	we move; you (all) move; they move
Future (AV)	I shall move; you will move; he, she, or it will move	we shall move; you (all) will move; they will move
Imperfect (AV)	I was moving, you were moving; he, she, or it was moving	we were moving; you (all) were moving; they were moving
Perfect (AV)	I moved; you moved; he, she, or it moved	we moved; you (all) moved; they moved
Future Perfect (AV)	I shall have moved, you will have moved; he, she, or it will have moved	we shall have moved; you (all) will have moved; they will have moved
Pluperfect (AV)	I had moved; you had moved; he, she, or it had moved	we had moved; you (all) had moved; they had moved
Present (PV)	I am moved; you are moved; he, she, or it is moved	we are moved; you (all) are moved; they are moved
Future (PV)	I shall be moved; you will be moved; he, she, or it will be moved	we shall be moved; you (all) will be moved; they will be moved
Imperfect (PV)	I was being moved; you were being moved; he, she, or it was being moved	we were being moved; you (all) were being moved; they were being moved

Noun Endings

In the student text on page 39 the three noun chant charts are listed. They are also on pages 42, 43, and 44. The boxes contain endings for nouns to indicate which case the noun is in and, therefore, its function in the sentence. A group of nouns with the same endings is called a declension or a noun family. There are five declensions in Latin with variations within some of those. Given here are the endings for the first and second declension and a variation of the second declension called the second declension *neuter*.

The charts on pages 42, 43, and 44 point out the endings for the nominative, genitive, dative, accusative and ablative cases respectively. The column headings indicate the singular and plural endings. The nominative case, used for the subject of a sentence, is the only one used by the students in the first year, although there will be some exposure to the other cases. Both the singular and plural forms will be used for much of the year. The nominative form is the basic form and that by which the nouns are listed in dictionaries and the word lists of this course. When a noun is serving in a sentence as something other than a subject, it is put in one of the remaining cases.

The second case, the genitive, is used to show possession. The genitive is also the case that indicates reliably what declension the noun is. For that reason, it is given *following* the nominative form in dictionaries. Beginning with week 18 on page 27, the form is listed on the word lists for nouns of the first and second declensions. If a noun is in the first declension, its genitive singular ending is *ae* and if it is in the second declension, its genitive singular ending is *i*.

The third case is the dative. Its main use is for indirect objects. The fourth case is the accusative. It is primarily used for direct objects and objects of some prepositions. It will be used extensively in the second year. The bottom case is the ablative and it has many uses, among them indication of manner, means, agent, place from which, separation, time when, etc. Not included in the chants are two less-used cases, the locative and vocative. You don't need to be concerned with them now.

Although the students will not be working with the cases in translating this year, it is good to have them learn the names of the cases. A mnemonic device used (and invented, I suspect) by my first Latin teacher is: **N**o **g**ood **d**ad **a**ttacks **a**pples. I confess to having used it myself. The kids enjoyed it.

Demonstrated on the next page are the endings used in forms of nouns of the corresponding declension and the translation of those forms. It is important for the students to realize that each nouns is in a certain declension. Sometimes they have the wrong idea at first that one can put a noun in any declension and then change its endings accordingly. As a general rule, if the noun ends in "a", it only takes the first declension endings. If the noun end in "us", it only takes the second declension endings.

Gender

Latin, like English, makes a distinction between three genders: masculine, feminine, and neuter. Nouns of the first declension are usually feminine. There are a few noun exceptions, of the first declension, representing people who had jobs that were traditionally male; e.g., *poēta*, poet; *nauta*, sailor; *agricola*, farmer. Most second declension masculine nouns have a singular (nominative) "us" ending, though a few end in "er".

First Declension (*a, ae, ae*)

Case	Singular		Plural	
Nom.	stell**a**	a star, the star, star	stell**ae**	the stars
Gen.	stell**ae**	of the star, the star's	stell**ārum**	of the stars, the stars'
Dat.	stell**ae**	to/for the star	stell**īs**	to/for the stars
Acc.	stell**am**	the star (direct object)	stell**ās**	the stars (direct object)
Abl.	stell**ā**	from/by/with, etc.,	stell**īs**	from/by/with, etc., stars

Notice that the endings are added to a base that does not change. If there is a change in the base, it will show up in the genitive form and will be given in the dictionary listing. Also, notice the variety of translations given for *stella*: a star, the star, star. The same flexibility applies to the other cases because classical Latin does not have a word for the articles *a, an,* and *the.* Context will also be important later in determining what case is being used when there is more than one possibility, such as in a word ending in *ae.* In the regular work for this year, the students are told that the only case used is the nominative, so they can conclude that if the ending is *ae,* it must be nominative plural. Remember, the nouns are listed in the nominative case with the genitive ending appearing after the comma. For example: lupus, i; saxum, i).

Second Declension (*us, i, o*)

Case	Singular		Plural	
Nom.	amic**us**	the friend	amic**i**	the friends
Gen.	amic**ī**	of the friend, the friend's	amic**ōrum**	the friends'
Dat.	amic**ō**	to/for the friend	amic**īs**	to/for the friends
Acc.	amic**um**	the friend (direct object)	amic**ōs**	the friends (direct object)
Abl.	amic**ō**	from/by/with, the friend	amic**īs**	from, etc., the friends

The difference between second declension and the pattern that follows on the next page, which is a variation of the second declension, is that the following one is for nouns of the second declension that are neuter in gender. Note the three forms where there is a difference between the two. In all neuter declensions, the nominative singular and accusative singular endings will always be the same. Likewise, the nominative plural and accusative plurals endings will always be the same. All the nouns on the word lists that end in *-um* are neuter nouns that will follow this declension

Second Declension Neuter (*um, i, o*)

Case	Singular			Plural	
Nom.	verb**um**	the word		verb**a**	the words
Gen.	verb**i**	of the word, the word's		verb**orum**	of the words
Dat.	verb**o**	to/for the word		verb**is**	to/for the words
Acc.	verb**um**	the word (direct object)		verb**a**	the words (direct object)
Abl.	verb**o**	from/by/with, etc., word		verb**is**	from, etc., the words

Pronouns

The remaining chants on pages 40 and 45 of the student text are complete pronouns declined. The first two are Latin for "this" and "these". The third and fourth are the declension of the pronouns for the first person and second person.

A word about order: all the chants are meant to be recited starting at the top left proceeding through each box by descending through first the left column and then the right, then going on to the next box. The exceptions to this are *hic, haec, hoc (pg. 31)*, *hi, hae, haec (pg. 32)*, and *ego, meī, mihi (pg. 33)*. The arrows lead the way through the chant.

Below and on the following page are the translations of these pronouns. The students will not learn their translation this year, except for perhaps the general meaning.

Singular Pronoun *(hic, haec, hoc)*

	Masculine	Feminine	Neuter		
Nom	hic	haec	hoc		this
Gen	huius	huius	huius		of this
Dat.	huic	huic	huic		to, for this
Acc.	hunc	hanc	hoc		this
Abl.	hōc	hāc	hōc		from, etc., this

120

Plural Pronoun (*hī, hae, haec*)

	Masculine	Feminine	Neuter	
Nom	hī	hae	haec	these
Gen	hōrum	hārum	hōrum	of these
Dat.	hīs	hīs	hīs	to, for these
Acc.	hōs	hās	haec	these
Abl.	hīs	hīs	hīs	from, etc., these

The reason there are three Latin words for a single English meaning is that a different one is used depending on whether the noun designated is masculine, feminine, or neuter.

Prounouns I and us, you and we (*ego, mei, mihi*)

Case	Singular				Plural	
Nom.	ego	I			nōs	we
Gen.	meī	of me			nostrum	of us
Dat.	mihi	to/for me			nōbīs	to/for us
Acc.	mē	me	CHANT		nōs	us
Abl.	mē	from, etc. me	FLOW		nōbīs	from, etc., us
Nom.	tu	you			vōs	you (plural)
Gen.	tui	of you			vestrum	of you
Dat.	tibi	to / for you			vōbis	to/for you
Acc.	te	you			vōs	you
Abl.	te	from, etc.,			vōbīs	from, etc. you

These prounouns are used the same way as the nouns that they replace, with a couple of exceptions. The nominative forms are only used for emphasis, since the verb tells who the subject is without a separate pronoun being necessary. (*vocat* = he calls) The other difference is that the genitive form is not used to show possession; a separate adjective is used instead.

DERIVATIVES

A derivitative is not an "original" word, but one that comes directly from another word (from roots meaning "to flow downstream from" a source).

Latin	English	Derivative
māter	mother	maternal

The basic guidelines for determining if an English word is a derivative of a certain Latin word are:

1)   In part or in whole, they have similar spellings.

2)   They have *some* of the same meaning.

These are not foolproof tests—some words appear to be unlikely descendants, but in fact are, while others present themselves as heirs and are not. Discerning likely derivatives requires practice throughout the year. Some students take to it quickly; others need practice in applying the two little tests above. Working with derivatives is a good path to the growth of English vocabulary. It is also helpful for memorizing Latin vocabulary when the meaning of an English derivative is already known, and it is preferable to memorization based on fiction such as "I praise loudly" to help one remember the meaning of *laudo*. You may also find more derivatives in the Latin entries of our Latin dictionary.

Working with derivatives should be part of the weekly routine. Included in the weekly lessons, at the end of each lesson in the teacher's book, are lists of derivatives for each week. The lists are not exhaustive, but include words which will be most useful. There are more words in the list than you will want to use, so some are for your reference rather than the students' use. Beginning on page 108 of the student book, are pages to list derivatives you discuss together each week. It's good practice for the students to come up with derivatives after considering the Latin words for each week.

Derivatives
(This worksheet is found on pg. 108 in the Student Book.)

- Use these Latin words and your sharp brain to match the English words to their definitions.

vir	man	vivō	I live	nihil	nothing
amicus	friend	terra	land or earth	laudō	I praise
puer	boy	sol	sun	mare	sea
audiō	I hear	flūmen	river	house	home

- Find the definition for these English words by choosing the Latin word from which each is derived. When you have found its definition, write the Latin word in the blank. The first one is done for you.

1. amicable	a. worth of praise	laudable
2. flume	b. a sailor or seaman	mariner
3. mariner	**c. friendly**	**amicus**
4. vivacious	d. able to be heard	audible
5. laudable	e. one who believes nothing is worth believing in	nihilist
6. audible	f. having to do with the earth or its inhabitants	terrestrial
7. virile	g. having manly strength	virile
8. nihilist	h. immature, childish	puerile
9. parasol	i. an artificial channel for a stream of water	flume
10. puerile	j. lively	vivacious
11. terrestrial	k. having to do with the home or family	domestic
12. domestic	l. a light umbrella used for sun protection	parasol

WEEKLY LESSONS

Weekly Lessons

The weekly lessons are primarily for those teachers who do not use the video tape series.

Week 1

1. Introduce the word list for week 1, asking students to carefully imitate the pronunciation. Discuss the derivatives for the first three words on the list (amateur, video, captain).

2. Introduce the first chant: *amo, amas, amat, amamus, amatis, amant.* Most of the students will not do it perfectly the first time, so it will take some practice.

3. Have the students write the first quotation, taken from the bottom of the word list on the quotation page in the student book beginning on page 115. Since the "c" has a hard sound, it will be pronounced differently that it is in English usage. Show them the commonly used abbreviation *etc.* You may want to discuss why it is incorrect to write " and etc."

4. Derivatives: amateur, amatory, evident, vision, visible, vista, visit, visor, visual(the perfect passive participle of *video* is *visus*, which gives us most of the derivatives of *video*), chapter, cap, capital, cape (both kinds). An explanation for derivatives appears on page 122 of this text.

Week 2

1. Explain to the students that the Romance languages—Italian, French, Spanish, Portuguese, and Romanian—all came from the language of the Romans and therefore have much vocabulary that is very similar. You may want to use the Number Chart on page 104 of the student book and page 104 of this book, to show the simalarities.

2. Go over the meaning of the following chant, as arranged below.

	Singular	Plural			
1st person	amō	amāmus		I love	we love
2nd person	amas	amātis		you love	you (all) love
3rd person	amat	amant		he, she, it loves	they love

3. Once that is practiced and understood, have the students figure out the conjugated forms of *laudo*, starting with what they already know: laudo=I love.

	Singular			Plural	
1st person	laudō	laudāmus		I praise	we praise
2nd person	laudās	laudātis		you praise	you (all) praise
3rd person	laudat	laudant		he, she, it praises	they praise

4. It will be one step farther for them to translate the chant for this week: This is an irregular verb, not following the pattern of any conjugation, and one does not add or drop endings from a stem. There is some resemblance in the end of the words to endings already encountered in the first conjugation.

	Singular			Plural	
1st person	sum	sumus		I am	we are
2nd person	es	estis		you are	you (all) are
3rd person	est	sunt		he, she, it is	they are

5. On section "E" of the student worksheet, the spanish word for "friend" is amigo. Show the similarity between *amīcus* and amigo.

6. After introducing the quotation *Cave Canem*, "Beware of the dog", translate each word separately (cave=beware, canem=dog). This will be an introduction to one of the major differences between Latin and English: the endings of Latin words change much more than English. You've seen this already in the conjugation of verbs, but the difference is greater in nouns. It is probably enough for now to point out to the students (or have them discover) that *canis* has a different ending here: *em* instead of *is*. This is because of the different function it has in the sentence. These changes in endings (inflection) do for Latin what word order does in English. Because of this, word order is much less important in Latin.

7. Derivatives: laud, laudatory, cogitate, vivacious, auditory, auditorium, audio, audible, amiable, amicable, puerile, virile, canine, maternity, maternal, paternal, domain, salvo, valor, value, valediction.

Week 3

1. Use the derivative worksheet on page 109 of the student book for all of the vocabulary covered in the first three weeks.

2. In the quotation, both *caelum* and *terram* are in the accusative case. This is because they are the direct objects of *creavit*. *Terram* can be pointed out to the students as another example of the ends of Latin words changing. Don't worry about getting the verb translated right. It's more important right now to learn the quote as a whole and the grammar will come later. Remember that *creo* is a first-conjugation verb, conjugating thus: *creo, creas, creat, creamus, creatis, creant.*

3. When working with the chant for this week, relate it to the previously learned *amo* chant. Notice that the o,s,t... endings are placed on the stem *ama*.

4. Derivatives: create, datum, clamor, deity, Lucifer, aviary, solar, parasol, solstice, lunar, marine, terrestrial, stellar, constellation, flume, Montana, mountebank, .mount, mountain, nihilist.

Week 4

1. Have the students complete Crossword 1 on pages 118 and 119 of the their book. The word list and answer key begins on page 168 of the this book.

2. This would be a good week to have the student begin distinguishing between 1st- and 2nd- conjugation verbs. Use those terms interchangeably with "a" and "e" conjugations. *Dirigo* is in the thirdconjugation; therefore, the students will not be expected to conjugate it.

3. Have the students sort the word list into nouns, verbs and adjectives as an exercise. (*Semper* won't be used.)

4. Ask the students to translate the chants from memory for first, second, and third person practice.

5. Derivatives: doctor, doctrine, document, docent, docile, demonstrate, portage, transportation, portable, important, export, deport, report, rapport, porter (the kind that carries luggage),labor, ludicrous, magistrate, discipline, disciple, library, libretto, librarian, bonus, magnify, magnanimous, magnificent, magnitude, magnum.

Week 5

1. Research the founding of Rome (encyclopedia, internet, library) and explain it to the student. A great deal of what you'll find is myth, but important to learn.

2. Derivatives: administration, mutant, mutable, immutable, mutate, orator, oracle, oration, retard, tardy, liberate, ocular, binocular, monocle, oculist, pedal, pedestrian, pedestal, pedometer, pedicure, millipede, pedigree, piedmont, pioneer (the genitive form of *pes* is *pedis*), brachial, oral, corpse, corps, manual, manicure, novice, novelty, malign, malignant, malevolence, malaria, malady, malpractice, malicious, malice.

3. You will find the Latin State Mottoes on page 105 of the student book and this book.

Week 6

1. *Scrībō, currō,* and *faciō* are third-conjugation verbs, so do not conjugate them.

2. If you haven't previously, begin using and having the students use the terms first, second and third person in reference to verbs. Review the section on page 105 regarding the use of person.

3. Derivatives: vocation, vocative, invoke, invocation, revoke, avocation, evoke, vouch, advocate, provoke, convocation, despair, scribble, scribe, describe, inscribe, script, scripture, transcribe, circumscribe, prescribe, subscribe, postscript, conscript, curriculum, curricle, current, currency, cursive, cursory, factory, fact, factor, facsimile, feminine, female, fraternal, fraternity, fraternize, fratricide, friar, sorority, nomenclature, nominate, noun, misnomer, pronoun, nominal, arbor, arboretum, sylvan, insulate, insulin, insular, peninsula, isle, subterranean, submarine, subarctic, subject, subordinate.

Week 7

1. This week is mainly used for reviewing in preparation for the test.

2. Derivatives: despair (*despero* itself comes form *spero*), expect, imperative, emperor, imperial, simulate.

3. Test 1 should be given at the end of this week.

Week 8

1. This is the first of seven weeks concentrating on the conjugation of second conjugation verbs. Help the students to see the similarities and differences between this conjugation and the firstconjugation.

2. With the introduction this week of *sedeō*, now would be a good time to begin the use of a few imperatives. To tell one person to do something, the present stem is used; to give a plural command, *–te* is added to that. So, to tell one person to sit, the imperative is *sede*. The plural imperative for it is *sedete*. Here are some additional commands you may find useful:

sta, state	stand
labora, laborate	work
cogita, cogitate	think
recita, recitate	read aloud
scribe, scribete	write

3. Derivatives: habit, able, habitable, habitat, inhabit, inhibit, exhibit, prohibit, habeas corpus, move, remove, mobile, motion, motive, commotion, emotion, promote, remote, valor, value, sedentary, session, obsess, preside, reside, navigate, navigable, patriot, expatriate, nautical, navy, naval, aquatic, aquarium, aqua, labor, vesper, nocturnal, exit, except, exclaim, excommunicate, exhale, exspect, extend.

Week 9

1. This would be a good time to check on the students' ability to write the chants from memory.

2. The word *cōpiae* (troops) is always plural. There is no singular form.

3. Derivatives: capture, captive, captivate, captivity, caption, captor, catch, except, timid, intimidate, terror, terrify, terrorist, invincible, vincible, vanquish, victor, convince, military, militia, equestrian, peril, copious, cornucopia, ignition, ignite, belligerent, bellicose, ante-bellum, gladiator, gladiola, castle, contradict, contrary, contrast, contraband, counterfeit, counterpoint, counterweight, counterclockwise.

130

Week 10

1. Please note, *scriptum* in the quotation is the passive participle of *scribere*. Although the student may not have a use for that kind of term, you may want to help them look ahead by telling them in the future when they learn a verb, they will need to learn four different forms of it. These four forms for *scribo* are *scribo, scribere, scripsi, scriptum.*

2. Derivatives: agent, agency, agenda, agitate, act, agile, regent, regiment, regime, correct, direct, debt, debit, legislature, legal, legitimate, vital, vitamin, vitality, viable, crux, crucify, crucial, homo sapiens, family, familial, familiar, filial, glory.

Week 11

1. The number chart is for use with this weeks lesson. It shows clearly the close relationship between the Romance languages and Latin. Often someone in the class will have already learned to count to ten in Spanish or French.

2. Derivatives: unity, uniform, union, unite, unicorn, unicycle, triune, unanimous, universe, unify, dual, deuce, triennial, trident, triceps, triangle, trimester, triple, tripod, tricycle, quatrain, quarter, quart, quartet, quadrille, quintuplet, octave, September, October, November, December, decimate, decimal, dime, Dixie, century, centennial, centurion, cent, millenium, impecunious, pecuniary, number, numerous, enumerate, paucity.

3. The derivation of "Dixie" from *decem* needs a story to explain it. The name was originally a nickname for New Orleans from the ten-dollar bill issued by a New Orleans bank before the Civil War. The bill was called a "dixie" because it had a large *Dix* printed on each side, *dix* being French for ten.

Week 12

1. It would be good to begin to establish with these simple sentences a pattern for translating Latin sentences. Begin with the verb. For the first sentence of C) on the worksheet, determine that *servat* means "he, she, or it saves", then have the students look for a noun that would tell who the he, she, or it is (*dominus*). In putting that information together in an English translation, point out that since *dominus* tells us specifically who the he, she or it is, we don't need to include the he, she, or it in the translation, thereore it would be "the Lord saves". It would also be good to teach the students to normally expect the verb at the end of a Latin sentence. Word order is not as rigid in Latin as it is in English, but that is the normal place for the verb.

2. In section "C", item number two, the word *mīles* is not in the first or second declension. The student does not need to worry about declining *mīles* in this book.

3. Derivatives: stance, statue, stature, circumstance, audacious, volley, volatile, posture, position, deposit, interpose, apposition, oppose, indubitable, dominate, domain, dominion, agriculture, serf, serve, service, servile, servitude, porter, portal, portcullis, mesa, ingratiate, gratitude, facility, facile, facilitate, adapt, add, adhere, adjacent, ad hoc, ad lib, admit.

4. In exercise "C," *servi* is from *servus* and it appears in the nominative plural case.

Week 13

1. Although there are no sentences with nouns on the worksheet for this week, additional practice would be good. Remember the translation order: First find the verb, then look for the subject (if there is one). Some possibilities:

Servus paret.	(The slave obeys.)
Filiae dolet.	(The daughters grieve.)
Magister monet.	(The teacher warns.)
Deus creat.	(God creates.)

2. Derivatives: tenant, tenacious, tenable, tenure, admonish, monitor, spectacles, spectacle, spectator, spectacular, expect, dolor, digit, digital, cordial, cordate, capillary, aural, face, mental, long, longitude, longevity (but not a derivative of *vita*), dulcimer, fortitude, fort, force, reinforce, pianoforte.

Week 14

1. Derivatives: delete, internecine, occupy, occupation, respond.

2. There is no quotation this week.

3. Test II should be given at the end of this week.

LATIN PRONUNCIATION AID TAPE

Welcome to the Canon Press, Mars Hill Series, of Latin text books.

This tape is designed to aid you in working through the Latin course books by providing a brief vocal guide for Latin pronunciation.

The first item you should note about Latin pronunciation is that it is not nearly as important as is sometimes thought. One reason is that you are not teaching the student conversational Latin. Unlike Spanish or French or other modern languages, no contemporary culture speaks Latin. The greatest value for most students is indirect, and pronunciation is not directly related to such benefits. In the long run, most students will encounter their Latin on the printed page.

Furthermore, since we didn't have tape recorders when Latin was spoken, Latin scholars themselves are divided over proper pronunciation. Some defend so-called "classical" pronunciation, others "ecclesiastical," and others prefer "Protestant" or "English" pronunciation, where the sounds are largely linked to the English vernacular. Our Latin text and the tape teach "classical" pronunciation. The one genuinely important point about pronunciation is consistency. As Dorothy Sayers advises, "Choose a pronunciation and stick with it."

So, though proper pronunciation is not vital to learning Latin, many people still feel somewhat lost without some pronunciation examples. For that reason, we have produced this tape.

This tape is designed for use with Canon Press's Latin Primer Book I. The tape works through every word listed in each of the twenty-seven lessons. In each lesson, the tape instructor will first pronounce each Latin word twice, then pause, and then read the English translation.

Teachers working through the text books on their own, may wish to go through the entire tape at once, trying to absorb the pronunciation patterns so that the teacher can lead students on their own without the tape. Alternatively, teachers may wish to use the tape lesson-by-lesson with the student listening to the tape. In this situation, students may listen to the Latin words pronounced twice, and, during the pause, they may repeat the Latin word and try to recall the English translation before the tape does.

Whatever way you use this tape, we hope it will aid you in your adventure in Latin!

Canon Press

P.O. BOX 8729, MOSCOW, ID 83843
800-488-2034

Week 15

1. Sentence practice:

Perīculum auget.	(The danger increases.)
Cīvis manet.	(The citizen remains.)
Aedificia manent.	(The buildings remain.)
Familia	(The household

You may want to try some in the future tense. By translating one example for them, some students will have all that they need to do others on their own.

Roma augebit.	(Rome will increase.)
Copiae manebunt.	(Troops will remain.)
Miles iuvabit.	(The soldier will help.)

2. Derivatives: communicate, communique, augment, auction, merit, remain, permanent, mansion, edifice, civil, civic, city, citizen, urban, suburban, urbane, via, viaduct, voyage, convey.

Week 16

1. It is now time to start applying the declension chants to whole nouns. If the endings were learned thoroughly when they were introduced and practiced daily, this should come easily to the students. Having examples of declined nouns that can be seen as they are recited makes the connection a small step. Since there is only one 1st-declension noun in this week, use earlier ones such as *via, Roma, porta, mensa, puella* and *terra* for practice.

terra	terrae		vicus	vicī
terrae	terrārum		vicī	vicōrum
terrae	terrīs		vicō	vicīs
terram	terrās		vicum	vicōs
terrā	terrīs		vicō	vicīs

2. *Moenia* is a 3rd-declension neuter noun existing only in the plural forms, so do not decline it now.

3. Derivatives: vicinity, captive, captivate, mural, intramural, prefect, campus, camp, compute, dispute, repute, prepare, pare, repair, recuperate, superable, insuperable, exercise, prince, principal, principle, vulnerable.

Week 17

1. Continue practicing declining nouns of the firstand seconddeclensions. Nouns in the firstdeclension from this week are: *iniuria, fama, sagitta, sica,* and *pugna.* Nouns in the second declension are *nuntius, triumphus,* and *legatus.* (*Exercitus* is in the 4th declension.)

iniūria	iniūriae	nuntius	nuntiī
iniūriae	iniūriārum	nuntiī	nuntiōrum
iniūriae	iniūriīs	nuntio	nuntiīs
iniūriam	iniūriās	nuntium	nuntiōs
iniūriā	iniūriīs	nuntiō	nuntiīs

2. You may want to mention the word "incognito" in connection with the quotation.

3. Derivatives: announce, denounce, pronounce, renounce, injury, triumph, fame, famous, defame, pugnacious, legate, legation, hostile, noxious, innocent, nocuous, innocuous, nuisance, perturb, fierce, antiquity, antique.

Week 18

1. Now that the genitive endings of 1st- and 2nd-declension nouns are given on the word lists, the students can discern with certainty when a noun is in one of those declensions. (1st-declension nouns have *ae* for the genitive ending; seconddeclension nouns have *i*.) Keep practicing the declining of nouns and the names of the cases.

regina	reginae		colonus	colonī
reginae	reginārum		colonī	colonōrum
reginae	reginīs		colonō	colonīs
reginam	reginās		colonum	colonōs
reginā	reginīs		colono	colonīs

2. Derivatives: population, populous, populace, people, public, popular, colony, colonial, social, sociable, society, associate, corona, coronation, coronary, coronet, coroner, crown, duke, duchess, duchy, gens, Gentile, gentle, gentry, probation, probe, probable, probate, negate, negative, legate, delegate, relegate, legacy, allege, prohibit, recusant, non-, potent, potential, potentate, miser, miserable, misery.

Week 19

1. Sentence practice:

Herbae flōrent.	(The plants are flourishing.)
Lupus occultat.	(The wolf is hiding.)
Aura dēlectat.	(The breeze delights.)
Aquila bene videt.	(The eagle sees well.)
Herbae flōrebunt.	(The plants will flourish.)

2. Derivatives: lupus, lupine, nimbus, taurine, aura, herb, herbarium, herbaceous, herbicide, herbivore, spelunker, aquiline, flourish, floruit, occult, delectable, clandestine, benediction, benefactor, benevolent, benefit, benign, satisfy, satiate, insatiable, satisfaction.

3. Discuss the quotation: Note that Brutus was one of the conspiritors against Julius Caesar.

Week 20

1. All the words on this list are neuter nouns of the seconddeclension, so they all follow the chant for this week.

verbum	verba		folium	folia
verbī	verbōrum		foliī	foliōrum
verbō	verbīs		foliō	foliīs
verbum	verba		folium	folia
verbō	verbīs		foliō	foliīs

2. Derivatives: verb, adverb, proverb, verve, donate, donor, condone, pardon, sign, signal, signature, significant, insignia, designate, regnal, interregnum, regnant, pabulum, escutcheon, stagnate, stagnant, auxiliary, premium, benefice, beneficiary, foliage, defoliate, foliation, foil, folio, portfolio.

Week 21

1. It will probably take at least two weeks to cover this material and to prepare for the test. There is no quotation this week.

2. This week have students do Crossword II on page 120 of the student book. The crossword puzzle and answer key begins on page 170 of this book.

3. In addition to the constellations listed in the word list, have the students translate from the list of constellations on page 106 in their book, and page 106 of this book.

4. Derivatives: ursine, scorpion, level, deliberate, equilibrium, aurora, lion, leonine, piscary, piscine, porpoise, virgin, cancer, canker, major, minor.

5. Test III should be given at the end of review.

Week 22

1. Extra sentences:

Avus recitabit.	(The grandfather will read aloud.)
Nuntius errat.	(The messenger is wandering.)
Discipīna parat.	(The training prepares.)
Adulēscēns non rogabit.	(The young man will not ask.)
Populi improbi non	(Wicked nations do not flourish.)

   Note in the last sentence that the ending of the adjective has changed from its basic form. This is so that the adjective matches the noun it modifies in gender, number, and case. Point out to the students that it can have different endings. Word order is something that can also be observed. The main point to remember is that word order in Latin is less important to the meaning than it is in English.

2. This chant is easiest to memorize and use if one starts with *hic* and proceeds across each row (*hic, haec, hoc, huius, huius, huius, huic.*).

3. The quotation is from Descartes.

4. Derivatives: appellation, interrogate, prerogative, error, err, erratic, aberration, recite, recital, placebo, placid, please, pleasant, complacent, adolescent, animal, animosity, animus, equanimity, magnanimous, pusillanimous, unanimous, discipline, beatitude, beatific, stultify, honest, content.

Week 23

1. This chant is done in the same order as last week's. (across each row)

2. Derivatives: anchor, vent, ventilate, velum, undulate, tempest, itinerant, itinerary, class, port, pontoon, punt (the boat), equal, equable, equate, equator, equity, equilateral, equivalent, equivocal, latitude, propinquity, approach.

Week 24

1. Continue reinforcing the difference between nouns, verbs, and adjectives. Both definitions and identifying traits in Latin can be used. For example, an adjective describes a noun or a pronoun and a Latin adjective usually has three different endings, which are listed in the dictionary.

2. Sentence practice:

Ecclēsia crēdat.	(The church believes.)
Christus līberat..	(Christ sets free.)
Ecclēsia superabit.	(The church will conquer.)
Christus est Dominus.	(Christ is Lord.)

3. The smoothest way to recite this week's chant is marked with gray arrows in the student book.

4. Derivatives: apostle, penalty, penal, Evangel, evangelical, evangelist, ecclesia, ecclesiastic, pacify, pacifist, pacific, mortal, mortgage, mortician, mortify, post-mortem, fidelity, infidel, faith, very, veracious, verify, verdict, verity, vivify, vivisection, vivarium, viper, creed, credit, credible, incredible, credence, credential, miscreant, credulous, predicate.

Week 25

1. *Sic Semper Tyrannis* is the motto of Virginia. It was also shouted by John Wilkes Booth after he assassinated President Lincoln.

2. *Serō* is in the 3rd-conjugation.

3. Sentence practice:

Agricola parat.	(The farmer prepares.)
Hortus florebit.	(The garden will flourish.)
Lupus vulnerat et necat.	(The wolf wounds and
Pastor clamat.	(The shepherd is shouting.)
Cibi delectant.	(The foods delight.)

4. Declension practice:

fossa	fossae		hortus	hortī
fossae	fossārum		hortī	hortōrum
fossae	fossīs		hortō	hortīs
fossam	fossās		hortum	hortōs
fossā	fossīs		hortō	hortīs

vinum	vina
vinī	vinōrum
vinō	vinīs
vinum	vina
vinō	vinīs

5. Derivatives: villa, village, horticulture, orchard, stable, fosse, wine, vine, vineyard, vintage, vinegar, animal, famine, famish, pastor, pastoral, semen, pulverize, powder, albino, albumen, auburn (which is odd), vulnerable.

Week 26

1. In 312, Constantine defeated his rival Maxentius at the Milvian Bridge and so became ruler of the western Roman empire. According to legend, before the battle he saw a cross in the sky and the words *in hoc signo vinces*. He then had his soldiers' shields marked with a monogram representing Christ had as his standard that monogram combined with the cross.

2. Derivatives: ire, irascible, irate, forum, forensic, language, lingo, lingua, linguist, linguistics, bilingual, sentence, sententious, vocal, voice, vowel, equivocal, republic, real, re, rebus, postulate, expostulate, inevitable, census, censor, alien, mediocre, interim, interior, internal, interrupt, international.

Week 27

1. Derivatives: annual, annuity, anniversary, biennium, millennium, perennial, tempo, temporal, temporary, temporize, contemporary, hour, menstrual, ancient, antecedent, antedate, anteroom, postgraduate, posterior, preposterous, procrastinate, multitude, multiple, premier, primal, primary, primate, prime, primitive, science, omniscience, conscience, conscious, final, finale, finish.

2. Test IV should be given at the end of this week.

TESTS

Test I

1) Translate these words into English.

pater	_____	caput	_____
soror	_____	sum	_____
mater	_____	vīvō	_____
insula	_____	sub	_____
arbor	_____	discipulus	_____
corpus	_____	manus	_____
canis	_____	stella	_____
lux	_____	flūmen	_____
magister	_____	oculus	_____
novus	_____	bonus	_____
magnus	_____	vir	_____
sōl	_____	nomen	_____
fēmina	_____	domus	_____
mare	_____	liber	_____
mons	_____	caelum	_____
frater	_____	terra	_____
puella	_____	Deus	_____
puer	_____	audiō	_____

2) Translate these words into Latin.

and _____   *always* _____

friend _____   *moon* _____

3) Give one derivative for each of the following words.

portō _____   sōl _____

clamō _____   mare _____

4) Translate these verbs into English.

mūtō _____   laudātis _____

ōrant _____   exspectās _____

dō _____   tardāmus _____

cogitat _____   administrās _____

vocat _____   amāmus _____

simulātis _____   dēsperant _____

5) Give the English translations for these Latin quotations.

• "et cetera": _____

• "Dum spiro, spero" _____

• "Cave canem":_____

• "In principio creavit Deus caelum et terram": _____

_____

6) Write the chants in the boxes.

amō	

sum	

ō	

bō	

bam	

Extra Credit: List three of the five Romance languages.

Test II

A) Translate the following words:

ignis	_____	filia	_____
patria	_____	filius	_____
labor	_____	diēs	_____
ager	_____	nox	_____
silva	_____	gladius	_____
auris	_____	nunc	_____
pecūnia	_____	porta	_____
king	_____	nauta	_____
mensa	_____	facilis	_____
perīculum	_____	cōpiae	_____
mens	_____	dulcis	_____
cor	_____	digitus	_____
navis	_____	equus	_____
fortis	_____	occupō	_____
water	_____	ad	_____
mīles	_____	longus	_____

B) Translate these numbers.

centum _____   mille _____

ūnus _____   decem _____

octō _____   trēs _____

duo _____   quattor _____

C) Give one derivative for three of the following words.

miles _____   ignis _____

vita _____   mens _____

D) Conjugate these verbs.

pareō	

necō	

E) Translate these verbs.

habēmus _____   spectat _____

servant _____   audētis _____

stō _____   timent _____

terrēs _____   volat _____

vincō _____   respondēs _____

sedētis _____   *we owe* _____

F) Translate these quoations.

- "E pluribus unum"   _____

- "Gloria in excelsis Deo"   _____

- "ante bellum"   _____

- "post scriptum"   _____

- "Anno Domini"   _____

- "Ex libris"   _____

G) Complete these chants.

a	

videō	

Test III

A. Give the English translation of these words.

nuntius	_____	donum	_____
moenia	_____	beneficium	_____
iniūria	_____	regnum	_____
corōna	_____	urbs	_____
taurus	_____	via	_____
nimbus	_____	aedificium	_____
exercitus	_____	aurōra	_____
geminus	_____	leō	_____
verbum	_____	piscis	_____
auxilium	_____	māior	_____
saxum	_____	potens	_____
pābulum	_____	bene	_____
folium	_____	clam	_____
spēlunca	_____	oppidum	_____

B. Translate these verbs.

nocent _____   merent _____

pertubāmus _____   communicās _____

augētis _____   recuperātis _____

dēlectat _____   superat _____

occultās _____   parāmus _____

exerceo _____   iuvō _____

C. Give a derivative for each word.

satis _____   miser _____

D. Translate these sentences.

• Coloni flōrent.   _____

• Sagittārius recusat.   _____

E. Change these nouns from singular to plural and then translate what you've written.

	Plural	**Plural**
praeda	_____	_____
captīvus	_____	_____
mūrus	_____	_____
regina	_____	_____
signum	_____	_____
scūtum	_____	_____

F. Translate these verbs into Latin.

he denies _____   they remain _____

G. Translate these quotations.

- cum laude

  _____

- Veni, vidi, vici

  _____

- Terra incognita

  _____

Test IV

A) Translate these words.

tempestās _____   pons _____

classis _____   animus _____

appellō _____   beātus _____

agricola _____   fossa _____

sēmen _____   evangelium _____

pax _____   ecclēsia _____

vox _____   mīrus _____

mediocris _____   mensis _____

annus _____   tempus _____

B) Translate these verbs.

sciō _____   crēdō _____

vītabunt _____   rogabit _____

censētis _____

C) Translate these sentences.

- Cibi placent. _____

- Adulēscēns nabit. _____

- Avus est honestus. _____

- Pastor recitat. _____

- Contentus sum. _____

D) Give a derivative of each of these Latin words.

errō _____   ventus _____

iter _____   lingua _____

annus _____

E) Translate the following:

- Deo volente _____

- Iesus, Rex Iudaecorum _____

- post meridiem _____

- Sic semper tyrannis _____

- ante meridiem _____

- In hoc signo vinces _____

- Cogito ergo sum _____

F) Complete this chant.

ego	

tu	

Test I (Key)

1) Translate these words into English.

pater	father	caput	head
soror	sister	sum	O a,
mater	mother	vīvō	I live
insula	island	sub	below
arbor	tree	discipulus	student
corpus	body	manus	hand
canis	dog	stella	star
lux	light	flūmen	river
magister	teacher	oculus	eye
novus	new	bonus	good
magnus	large	vir	man
sōl	sun	nomen	name
fēmina	woman	domus	house or home
mare	sea	liber	book
mons	mountain	caelum	sky or the heavens
frater	brother	terra	land or earth
puella	girl	Deus	God
puer	boy	audiō	I hear

2) Translate these words into Latin.

and	et	always	semper
friend	amicus	moon	luna

3) Give one derivative for each of the following three of these words.

portō	portable, porter	sōl	solar, solstice
clamō	clamor, exclaim	mare	marine, submarine

4) Translate these verbs into English.

mūtō	I change	laudātis	you (all) praise
ōrant	they prey	exspectās	you wait for
dō	I give	tardāmus	we delay
cogitat	he, she, or it thinks	administrās	you help or manage
vocat	he calls	amāmus	we love
simulātis	you (all) pretend	dēsperant	they despair of

5) Give the English translations for these Latin quotations.

- "et cetera":   and the rest

- "Dum spiro, spero"   While I breathe, I hope

- "Cave canem":   Beware of the dog

- "In principio creavit Deus caelum et terram":

    In the beginning God created the heavens and the earth.

6) Write the chants in the boxes.

amō	amāmus
amās	amātis
amat	amant

sum	sumus
es	estis
est	sunt

ō	mus
s	tis
t	nt

bō	bimus
bis	bitis
bit	bunt

bam	bamus
bas	batis
bat	bant

Extra Credit: List three of the five Romance languages.

Italian, Spanish, French, Romanian, Portugese

Test II (Key)

A) Translate the following words:

ignis	fire	filia	daughter
patria	native land	filius	son
labor	work, toil	diēs	day
ager	field	nox	night
silva	forest	gladius	sword
auris	ear	nunc	now
pecūnia	money	porta	door, gate
king	*rex*	nauta	sailor
mensa	table	facilis	easy
perīculum	danger	cōpiae	troops
mens	mind	dulcis	sweet
cor	heart	digitus	finger
navis	ship	equus	horse
fortis	strong, brave	occupō	I seize
water	*water*	ad	to, toward
mīles	soldier	longus	long

B) Translate these numbers.

centum	a hundred	mille	a thousand
ūnus	one	decem	ten
octō	eight	trēs	three
duo	two	quattor	four

C) Give one derivative for three of the following words.

mīles	military, militant	ignis	ignite, igneous, ignition
vīta	vitamin, vital, vitality	mens	mental, mentality

D) Conjugate these verbs.

pareō	parēmus
parēs	parētis
paret	parent

necō	necāmus
necās	necātis
necat	necant

E) Translate these verbs.

habēmus	we have or hold	spectat	he looks at
servant	they save	audētis	you (all) dare
stō	I stand	timent	they fear
terrēs	you frighten	volat	he, she, or it flies
vincō	I conquer	respondēs	you answer
sedētis	you (all) sit	*we owe*	debēmus

F) Translate these quotations.

- "E pluribus unum" — One out of many
- "Gloria in excelsis Deo" — Glory to God in the highest
- "ante bellum" — before the war
- "post scriptum" — written afterwards
- "Anno Domini" — In the year of our Lord
- "Ex libris" — From the books

G) Complete these chants.

a	ae
ae	ārum
ae	īs
am	ās
ā	īs

videō	vidēmus
vidēs	vidētis
videt	vident

Test III (Key)

A) Give the English translation of these words.

nuntius	message or messenger	donum	gift
moenia	forifications, walls of a city	beneficium	kindness
iniūria	injury	regnum	kingdom
corōna	crown	urbs	city
taurus	bull	via	road or way
nimbus	cloud	aedificium	building
exercitus	army	aurōra	dawn
geminus	twin	leō	lion
verbum	word	piscis	fish
auxilium	help, aid	māior	greater
saxum	rock	potens	powerful
pābulum	fodder, food for animals	bene	well
folium	leam	clam	secretly
spēlunca	cave	oppidum	town

B) Translate these verbs.

nocent	they harm	merent	they deserve
pertubāmus	we confuse	communicās	you share
augētis	you (all) increase	recuperātis	you (all) recover
dēlectat	he, she, or it delights	superat	he, she, or it conquers
occultās	you hide	parāmus	we prepare
exerceo	I train	iuvō	I help

C) Give a derivative for each word.

satis   satisfy, satisfaction   miser   miser, miserable

D) Translate these sentences.

• Coloni flōrent.   The settlers flourish.

• Sagittārius recusat.   The archer refuses.

E) Change these nouns from singular to plural and then translate what you've written.

	Plural	**Translation**
praeda	praedae	booties
captīvus	captīvi	captives
mūrus	mūri	walls
regina	reginae	queens
signum	signa	signs
scūtum	scūta	shields

F) Translate these verbs into Latin.

he denies   negat   they remain   manent

G) Translate these quotations.

- cum laude   with praise

- Veni, vidi, vici   I came, I saw, I conquered

- Terra incognita   Unknown land

Test IV (Key)

A) Translate these words.

tempestās	weather, storm	pons	bridge
classis	fleet	animus	mind
appellō	I name	beātus	blessed, happy
agricola	farmer	fossa	ditch
sēmen	seed	evangelium	good news
pax	peace	ecclēsia	church
vox	voice	mīrus	strange, wonderful
mediocris	ordinary	mensis	month
annus	year	tempus	time

B) Translate these verbs.

sciō	I know	crēdō	I believe
vītabunt	they will avoid	rogabit	he will ask
censētis	you (all) estimate		

C) Translate these sentences.

- Cibi placent.

  The foods please.

- Adulēscēns nabit.

  The young man will swim.

- Avus est honestus.

  The grandfather is honorable.

- Pastor recitat.

  The sheperd reads aloud.

- Contentus sum.

  I am satisfied.

D) Give a derivative of each of these Latin words.

errō — error, erroneous   ventus — vent, ventilate

iter — itinerary, itenerant   lingua — linguist

annus — annual, anniversary

E) Translate the following:

- Deo volente

  God willing

- Iesus, Rex Iudaecorum

  Jesus, King of the Jews

- post meridiem

  after noon

- Sic semper tyrannis

  Thus always to tyrants

- ante meridiem

  before noon

- In hoc signo vinces

  In this sign you will conquer

- Cogito ergo sum

  I think, therefore I am

F)   Complete this chant.

ego	nōs
meī	nostrum
mihi	nōbīs
mē	nōs
mē	nōbīs

tu	vōs
tuī	vestrum
tibi	vōbīs
tē	vōs
tē	vōbīs

CROSSWORD PUZZLES

Crossword I

Across		**Down**	
1	I shout	2	I praise
2	Light	3	I show
3	I direct	6	moon
4	I love	11	little
5	God	20	I give
6	I work	21	big
7	school *or* game	22	sea
8	nothing	23	earth, land
9	and	24	I teach
10	girl student	25	I see
11	I carry	26	girl
12	bird	27	star
13	sky	28	sun
14	always	29	mountain
15	I am	30	boy
16	friend	31	river
17	good	32	dog
18	book	33	man teacher
19	father	34	game *or* school

Crossword I

	1 C	L	A	22 M	O											
				A			24 D		2 L	U	X					
		3 D	I	R	I	G	O		A							32 C
		E		E			C		U							A
	4 A	M	O				E		5 D	E	U	28 S				N
		O		6 L	A	B	O	R	O			O				I
		N		U								7 L	U	D	U	S
		S		8 N	I	H	I	34 L								
	9 E	T		A				U								33 M
		R						10 D	I	27 S	C	I	30 P	U	L	A
	11 P	O	R	T	O			U		T			U			G
	A							S		E			E			I
	R									L			R			S
12 A	V	I	S				13 C	A	E	L	U	29 M		31 F		T
	U				23 T					A		O		L		E
	14 S	E	21 M	P	E	R						N		U		R
			A		R							15 S	U	M		
			G		R		25 V		26 P					E		
	20 D		N		16 A	M	I	C	U	S				N		
17 B	O	N	U	S			D		E							
			S				E		18 L	I	B	E	R			
							O		L							
								19 P	A	T	E	R				

Crossword II

Down		Across	
1	building	1	you all increase
2	kingdoms	15	you delight
3	road	22	we refuse
4	leader	28	well
5	breeze	33	I stand
6	herbs	40	I confuse
7	mountain	43	he hides
8	crowns	44	he trains
9	pair of scales	45	I write
10	bulls	46	you all help
11	weapons	47	they attack
12	partner	48	she shares
13	eagle	49	I order
14	charioteers	50	I do
15	lord or master	51	it flourishes
16	lion	52	he sets free
17	water-carrier	53	I give
18	captive	54	they approve
19	soldier	55	you hope
20	scorpion	56	I think
21	twins	57	I conquer
22	queens	58	you prepare
23	female bear	59	they give
24	wall	60	they prevent
25	northern	61	he deserves
26	caves	62	I appoint
27	towns	63	we harm
28	kindness	64	you find out
29	leaves	65	I see
30	message	66	they fear
31	city	67	you all remain
32	dawn	68	you deny
33	shield		
34	arrows		
35	silence		
36	word		
37	gifts		
38	enemy		
39	help, aid		
40	rewards		
41	camp		
42	citizen		

- What is the only word in the "down" list that is not a noun? _Northern (adjective)_

- What is the only word in the "across" list that is not a verb? _well (adverb)_

Crossword II

AUGETIS · OCCULTA · EXERCET · SCRIBO · IUVA · OPPUGNANT · COMMUNIC·AT · DELECT·AS · IUBEO · AGO · FLORET · LIBERAT · REC·USA·MUS · PRO·BANT · SPERA · PUT · SUPERO · BENE · PARAS · DANT · PROHIBENT · MERET · LEGO · NOCEMUS · PERTURBO · EXPLORAS · VIDEO · TIMENT · MANETIS · MEGAS

WORD LISTS

Nouns of the First and Second Declensions

(The number beside each word indicates the word list to which the word is assigned.)

First Declension:

agricola, ae	25	glōria	10	porta, ae	12
ancora, ae	23	grātiae	12	praeda, ae	16
aqua, ae	8	herba	19	puella, ae	2
aquila, ae	19	Hispānia	15	pugna, ae	17
aura, ae	19	hora, ae	27	rēgīna, ae	18
aurīga, ae	21	iniūria, ae	17	ripa, ae	19
aurōra, ae	21	insula, ae	6	Rōma, ae	15
Biblia Sacra	24	īra, ae	26	sagitta, ae	17
cōpiae, arum	9	Italia	15	sententia, ae	26
corōna, ae	18	lībra, ae	21	sīca, ae	17
disciplīna, ae	22	lingua, ae	26	silva, ae	6
discipula, ae	4	lūna	3	spēlunca, ae	19
ecclēsia, ae	24	magistra, ae	4	stella, ae	3
fāma, ae	17	mensa, ae	12	terra, ae	3
familia, ae	10	nauta, ae	8	toga, ae	26
fēmina, ae	6	ōra, ae	23	unda. ae	23
fīlia, ae	10	patientia, ae	22	ursa, ae	21
fossa, ae	25	patria, ae	8	via, ae	15
Gallia	15	pecūnia	11	villa, ae	25
Germānia	15	poena, ae	24	vīta, ae	10

- Second Declension

aedificium, ī	15	evangelium, ī	24	sacculus, ī	26
ager, agrī	12	fīlius, ī	10	sagittārius, ī	21
amicus, ī	2	folium, ī	20	saxum, ī	20
animus, ī	22	forum, ī	26	scorpius, ī	21
annus, ī	27	geminus, ī	21	scūtum, ī	20
apostolus, ī	24	gladius, ī	9	servus, ī	12
aquarius, ī	21	hortus, ī	25	signum, ī	20
auxilium, ī	20	lēgātus, ī	17	silentium, ī	20
avus, ī	22	liber, librī	4	socius, ī	18
bellum, ī	9	lūdus, ī	4	sōlum, ī	12
beneficium, ī	20	lupus, ī	19	stabulum, ī	25
bracchium, ī	5	magister, magistrī	4	stagnum, ī	20
caelum, ī	3	mūrus, ī	16	taurus, ī	19
campus, ī	16	nimbus, ī	19	tēlum, ī	20
capillus, ī	13	numerus, ī	11	triumphus, ī	17
captīvus, ī	16	nuntius, ī	17	ursus, ī	21
castellum, ī	9	oculus, ī	5	vēlum, ī	23
castra, ōrum	16	oppidum, ī	15	ventus, ī	23
Christus, ī	24	pābulum, ī	20	verbum, ī	20
cibus, ī	25	perīculum, ī	9	vīcus, ī	16
colōnus, ī	18	pīlum, ī	20	vīnum, ī	25
Dues, ī	3	populus, ī	18	vir, virī	2
digitus, ī	13	praefectus, ī	16		
discipulus, ī	4	praemium, ī	20		
dominus, ī	12	puer, puerī	2		
dōnum, ī	20	regnum, ī	20		
equus, ī	9	rēmus, ī	23		

Nouns of Other Declensions, Adjectives, Adverbs, et cetera

- Third Declension

adulēscēns	22	gens	18	ōs	5
animal	25	homō	10	pastor	25
arbor	6	hostis	17	pater	2
auris	13	ignis	9	pax	24
avis	3	iter	23	pēs	5
cancer	21	labor	8	piscis	21
canis	2	leō	21	pons	23
caput	1	lex	10	princeps	16
cīvis	15	lux	3	pulvis	25
classis	23	mare	3	rēx	10
collis	6	mater	2	sēmen	25
cor	13	mens	13	sōl	3
corpus	5	mensis	27	soror	6
crūs	5	mīles	9	tempestās	23
crux	10	moenia	16	tempus	27
dux	18	mons	3	urbs	15
famēs	25	mors	24	vesper	8
fīnis	27	navis	8	virgō	21
flūmen	3	nomen	6	vox	26
frāter	6	nox	8	vulnus	16

- Fourth and Fifth Declension

ariēs	21	fidēs	24	portus	23
diēs	8	Iesus	24	rēs	26
dōmus	2	manus	5	spēs	24
exercitus	17	merīdiēs	27		
faciēs	13	metus	9		

- Indeclinable

nihil	3

- Adjectives

aequus	23	fortis	13	novus	5
albus	25	honestus	22	octō	11
aliēnus	26	improbus	22	parvus	4
antīquus	17	lātus	23	paucī	11
austrālis	21	longus	13	potens	18
beātus	22	magnus	4	prīmus	27
bonus	4	māior	21	quattor	11
borēus	21	malus	5	quinque	11
centum	11	mediocris	26	septem	11
contentus	22	mille	11	sex	11
difficilis	12	minor	21	stultus	22
dulcis	13	mīrus	26	trēs	11
duo	11	miser	18	ūnus	11
facilis	12	multus	27	vērus	24
ferus	17	novem	11	vīvus	24

- Adverbs

bene	19	hodiē	27	satis	19
clam	19	non	18	semper	4
crās	27	nunc	10		
heri	27	saepe	8		

- et cetera

ad	12	ex	8	prope	23
ante	27	gratiās agō	13	sub	6
contrā	9	in	5	suprā	6
ecce	27	inter	26		
et	1	post	27		

Verbs

administro	5	floreo	19	probo	18
ago	10	habeo	8	prohibeo	18
amo	1	impero	7	puto	16
appello	22	iubeo	17	recito	22
audeo	12	iuvo	15	recuso	18
audio	2	laboro	4	recupero	16
augeo	15	laudo	2	rego	10
capio	9	lego	18	respondeo	14
censeo	26	libero	5	rogo	22
clamo	3	maneo	15	scio	27
cogito	2	mereo	15	scribo	6
communico	15	moneo	13	sedeo	8
credo	24	moveo	8	sero	25
creo	3	muto	5	servo	10

Verbs (continued)

curo	7	navigo	8	simulo	7
curro	6	neco	14	specto	13
debeo	10	nego	18	spero	6
delecto	19	no	23	sto	12
deleo	14	noceo	17	sum	2
demonstro	4	occulto	19	supero	16
despero	7	occupo	14	tardo	5
dirigo	4	oppugno	9	teneo	13
do	3	oro	5	terreo	9
doceo	4	pareo	13	timeo	9
doleo	13	paro	16	valeo	8
dubito	12	perturbo	17	video	1
erro	22	placeo	22	vinco	9
exerceo	16	pono	12	vito	26
exploro	19	porto	4	vivo	2
exspecto	7	postulo	26	voco	6
facio	6	praedico	24	volo	12
fleo	14	precor	10	vulnero	25